WELL OF LIES

The Walkerton Water Tragedy

COLIN N. PERKEL

M&S

National Library of Canada Cataloguing in Publication Data

Perkel, Colin N.
Well of lies: the Walkerton water tragedy

Includes index.
ISBN 0-7710-7019-5

1. Drinking water – Contamination – Ontario – Walkerton.
2. Water quality – Health aspects – Ontario – Walkerton.
3. Escherichia coli infections – Ontario – Walkerton.
4. Water quality management – Ontario – Walkerton. I. Title.

RA593.C3P47 2002   363.6'1'0971321   C2001-903787-2

Photographs supplied courtesy of The Canadian Press.

We acknowledge the financial support of the Government of Canada through the Book Publishing Industry Development Program for our publishing activities. We further acknowledge the support of the Canada Council for the Arts and the Ontario Arts Council for our publishing program.

Typeset by M&S, Toronto
Printed and bound in Canada
This book is printed on acid-free paper that is
100% ancient forest friendly (100% post-consumer recycled)

McClelland & Stewart Ltd.
The Canadian Publishers
481 University Avenue
Toronto, Ontario
M5G 2E9
www.mcclelland.com

1   2   3   4   5   06   05   04   03   02

WELL OF LIES

In Memory of:

Lenore Marie Al, Vera Coe, Evelyn Hussey,
Edith Pearson, Mary Rose Raymond, Laura Eva Rowe,
and Elizabeth Trushinski.

And to the people of Walkerton who suffered through so much.

Contents

Angel of Mercy, Angel of Death

Walkerton, Ontario, Canada
Saturday, May 20, 2000

TWENTY-TWO-MONTH-OLD Kody woke up violently ill, his diaper stained blood red. He kept throwing up. Tracey Hammell tended her only child while still trying to enjoy the sunshine as she indulged in that Canadian rite of spring known as the garage sale. Kody's sickness had actually begun two days earlier, and Tracey's mom had advised her to watch the boy and wait. She had heard there were other kids in the neighbourhood falling ill. Must be the flu going around, they thought. But Kody's condition this bright Saturday morning was getting worse. Tracey abandoned the knick-knacks on her front lawn and called the Walkerton hospital.

"Kody is like deathly ill and I thought it was the flu so I just left him, but he now needs to see someone," she told the nurse.

"What are his symptoms?"

Tracey described them.

"Well, we've got a waiting room full of people. So we won't be able to get to him right away."

"Then, when can I come? He's really sick. He needs to see somebody."

"Best to wait until four this afternoon. Just make sure you get fluids into him so he doesn't get dehydrated."

"But he won't drink."

"Do whatever you have to do to get it in him. Get a syringe."

And so Tracey Hammell got a medicinal syringe she had been using to give him Children's Tylenol, filled it from the kitchen tap, picked up her listless child, held his pale head back, and forced the water down his throat. Kody could barely register a protest. That afternoon, Tracey and her mom took Kody to the hospital. In the already crowded waiting room, she found herself sitting next to Stan Koebel's twenty-year-old son, Jacob. Stan, the hard-working, long-time manager of the Walkerton Public Utilities Commission, the man in charge of the town's water and electricity, wasn't there. Jacob was with a girlfriend, who had hurt her arm. Tracey knew him well. Her parents were old friends of Stan's parents. In years gone by, she had spent a lot of time babysitting Jacob and his sister, Stephanie, who now lived with her husband two doors down from the Hammells.

"I can't figure out why Kody's sick and he's throwing up and stuff," said Tracey to Jacob, making conversation. "I think it might be the flu."

"It's not the water," Jacob retorted. "My dad has been out all night flushing the system and he's been testing the water and it's not the water."

Tracey was struck dumb by the comment. The notion that water was causing Kody's illness had not entered her head. But her mom was curious.

"What do you mean, Jacob, it's not the water?"

"A few people are trying to accuse my dad of the water being bad," Jacob said sullenly.

As Dr. Paul McArthur examined Kody, Tracey asked him about the strange comment from Jacob.

"So what's this water thing I'm hearing out there?"

"There's no confirmation and I really shouldn't be saying anything, but I'm going to tell you: Please don't drink the water," McArthur responded.

He advised her to keep the youngster hydrated with bottled or sterilized water and to keep a close eye on him. The family went home. The next morning, Kody looked even more dreadful. He couldn't hold his head up. Her panic mounting, Tracey called the hospital.

"You've got to see him. He's lifeless. His eyes are rolling in the back of his head. He's just vomiting and has diarrhea every two minutes. He can't take it any more."

This time, the hospital told her to bring Kody in right away. A doctor examined him. Kody was obviously very ill, he told Tracey, but it wasn't clear what was ailing him. She asked if he could take some blood or run some tests, but the doctor demurred.

"He's not totally dehydrated yet. You have about four hours, so best to take him home."

"I've got four hours until he's totally dehydrated and you're sending him home again?" Tracy asked incredulously.

"Yes. We're really backed up here and there are no beds and we won't take an infant this age."

But the worried family insisted.

"We want to go somewhere where you can find a bed."

Minutes later, the doctor came back.

"There's a bed available in Guelph and there's one in Owen Sound," he said. "Your choice."

"Are we supposed to go on our own or what?" Tracey asked.

"Yep. Away you go," the harried doctor responded.

Tracey swallowed hard as the doctor retreated.

"Guess we'd better get going," she said to Kody.

The Hammells bundled the sick boy, who now suddenly seemed to be craving water, into the car and drove north forty-five minutes to Owen Sound.

"Why weren't you in here sooner?" the admitting nurse asked as soon as they arrived, her concern evident. "Why doesn't he have an IV hooked up?"

"They wouldn't do it in Walkerton," Tracey replied.

"That's just BS," the nurse said and immediately set about putting Kody on an IV without waiting for a doctor's instructions.

For three days, Kody lay in the pediatric ward at the Owen Sound hospital, until Dr. Ewan Porter, the pediatrician, told Tracey her toddler's kidneys were failing.

"He's a very sick boy," Porter said. "We can't do any more for him here. We're going to fly him to London."

Tracey had known that Kody was extremely ill, but until that moment, the unthinkable hadn't occurred to her.

"Can he die from this?" she asked the nurse as soon as Porter had left the room. "Do you think he can die from this?"

"Yes," the nurse replied. "It's very possible and things aren't looking good now."

"Can I go in the helicopter with him?" Tracey pleaded.

"I don't know if they'll let you go," the nurse said gently.

"If he's going to die, he's not going alone."

"You just tell them that," the nurse said.

As she tended to her son, Tracey's brother arrived. He was in tears. He motioned his parents aside and spoke softly to them.

"Why's Greg crying?" Tracey asked. "What's he so upset about?"

"He's just feeling bad for Kody," her mom soothed.

What she didn't tell her daughter was that Greg had just heard on the car radio while driving to the hospital that two-and-a-half-year-old Mary Rose Raymond, who lived in nearby Hanover, had died of E. coli bacterial poisoning. In Walkerton, fifty-six-year-old Betty Trushinski, who lived three houses down from the Hammells, had also heard about the girl's death. Health conscious and an avid water drinker, Trushinski had worked in the dietary department of the Walkerton hospital for twenty-five years. On the same day Tracey had taken little Kody to the hospital for the first time, Trushinski left work early because her stomach was hurting. She was still feeling poorly.

"Why couldn't it be somebody our age who's already had a full life?" she remarked to her husband, Frank, upon hearing that Mary Rose had died. "It's just not fair."

When the paramedics arrived to transport Kody, Tracy said, "I have to go with him. He's only a year and a half old. I have to go." The paramedics agreed. The whole family escorted Kody's gurney to the waiting red-and-white chopper. Tracey climbed in, too preoccupied to be nervous about her maiden helicopter flight. With the two paramedics on board, the pilot fired up the engines and a deafening noise filled the cabin. One of the paramedics handed Tracey a headset with a microphone. He gently placed a second set on the head of the unconscious little boy on the stretcher.

"Just keep talking to him," the paramedic told her. "He'll probably hear you."

As the helicopter roared into the sky on its flight to London, Tracey began talking.

"Kody, fight please," she said over and over. "I can't imagine my life without you." And in her head she kept thinking, You can't die. You can't die. Please don't die.

Four doctors were waiting when they arrived in London, and they set to work immediately. The child had blown up like a balloon. Even his long blond eyelashes had disappeared under the puffy lids of his seemingly lifeless blue eyes. So swollen were his little arms and legs that the doctors had trouble drawing blood and called in a cancer nurse to do the job. Once, Kody stirred and looked straight at his frantic mother.

"I'm okay, Mommy," he said before drifting back into blackness.

Dr. Doug Matsell, a kidney specialist, explained that Kody needed blood-cleansing dialysis to take over for his tiny non-functioning kidneys. They'd start in the morning, he said. Why not right away? Tracey asked. Matsell explained they didn't have the staff or an operating room. Not to worry. The nurses would keep an eye on him through the night. Tracey again summoned up all her nerve.

"Is he going to die or what?" she asked, the tremor in her voice belying her attempt at brave detachment.

Matsell took a long look at the petite blonde mother standing before him.

"Do you want me to tell you the truth, or do you want me to sugar-coat it?"

"I want the truth," she said, fighting back tears.

"It's a possibility," he said after a pause. "We'll do all we can."

Kody was put to bed upstairs, hooked up to all kinds of high-tech monitors, while his mom sat on a bed next to him.

"I'm okay, Mommy," Kody murmured at one point. "Get under the covers. I'm okay."

Tracey drifted off to sleep, praying for her child, only to be jolted awake at 4 A.M. by a cacophony of beeping machines, a hideous, electronic distress call. She took a few moments to orient herself in the gloom. Her husband, Kevin, bolted over from his bed. Kody was barely stirring. There was no hospital staff around. Tracey rushed out the door to look for help. She almost collided with two nurses running in from the other way.

"Excuse me, ma'am," said one. "You're going to have to step back. His heart is under stress."

Doug Matsell, responding to the page, hurried to examine Kody. We can't wait for a gurney, he said, nodding at Kevin. As soon as Kody had been detached from the various tubes and machines, Kevin picked up his son, and followed the doctor and nurses straight down to the pediatric critical care unit. There was no time to staff an operating room. They prepped the little boy, asked his parents to leave, drew the curtains around the bed, applied a local anesthetic, and performed the surgery right then and there to insert the dialysis tubes. To Matsell's consternation, Kody didn't even flinch when they sliced into his tummy.

The following day, Frank Trushinski drove his wife, Betty, back to the Walkerton emergency room, which had sent her home a day earlier. Her diarrhea had been bloody for three days now and her hands were swelling. This time, she was immediately admitted and soon transferred to London, where Frank and their three children kept a bedside vigil. Two days later, she began having difficulty breathing. Within another two days, the fifty-six-year-old was dead:

her brain, lungs, liver, kidneys, and intestines destroyed by the vicious verotoxin produced by E. coli O157:H7.

For two hellishly long weeks after the emergency operation, Kody's parents kept an almost constant watch by his bedside. He was hardly conscious, barely alive. Although his condition appeared to stabilize, it wasn't improving. Then he took a turn for the worse. The doctors had inserted the tubes, but the fluid wasn't draining as it should have done. Kody's blown-up stomach protruded like some grotesque pregnancy. He whimpered in pain, refusing to be touched. Once again, he went under the knife to have the tubes reinserted, this time in the operating room under full anesthetic. He improved almost immediately. Three days later, he was well enough to leave the critical care unit. An exhausted Matsell, who had barely left the hospital himself in weeks, prompting two of his own boys to visit him as he made his rounds, cracked a broad smile. It was a moment he would never forget:

"I can finally tell you: He's not going to die," he told Tracey.

Several days later, he told the relieved parents that Kody's bloodwork had shown remarkable improvement. The turnaround was so dramatic, in fact, that Matsell was inclined to be cautious. Just in case the lab had made a mistake, he said, he was going to have them run the blood tests again. They heard him returning even before he'd quite gotten through the door.

"Yippidee doo," he sang. "You did it, buddy! You finally made the turn!"

It was indeed as if a miracle had occurred, as if an angel had touched Kody. Matsell looked at a smiling Tracey.

"I'm not very religious," he said. "But there was something up above that helped."

On the day they arrived home in Walkerton, four weeks after their ordeal began, a grief-stricken Frank Trushinski walked down the sidewalk, past the house in which Stan Koebel's daughter lived, to welcome the Hammell family home.

"Betty is Kody's angel," he said.

PART ONE

BEFORE THE STORM

2

A Town and Its River

FROM ITS SOURCE in the Osprey Wetlands in the Dundalk highlands, one of the highest points in Ontario, the Saugeen River winds toward Lake Huron about two hundred kilometres to the west. The river, one of the larger ones in the province, gathers strength along the way, fed by numerous smaller creeks and waterways, several of which also have "Saugeen" in their names (derived from an Ojibwa word meaning "mouth of the river"). The gentle hills of Grey and then Bruce County overlook the river as it flows through Hanover directly east of Walkerton. Once a logger's paradise, much of the original bush has long been cleared, leaving small stands of maple, birch, cedar, and poplar that still feed area lumberyards. In the spring, deep winter snow melts away to reveal fields stubbled with last year's corn. This is primarily cattle country, mostly beef, but there are also dairy, sheep, pig, and poultry operations. In the sky above the ubiquitous round concrete silos topped with colourfully striped metal domes, Canada geese honk and turkey vultures search for carrion. Groundhogs peep from their burrows on roadside ditches as tired brown fields turn almost overnight to shimmering, verdant green, at times overlain with impossibly yellow dandelions. Freed from a seemingly endless winter of confinement, cattle graze contentedly, while songbirds search out a nest, occasionally choosing an unused roadside mailbox. In the mist of dusk, a horse-drawn buggy clatters purposefully along the gravel shoulder of the highway, just a metre or so from the trucks and cars whizzing by. At the reins, a bearded, black-clad Old Order Mennonite heads toward a destination he'll never seem to reach. It's hard to tell if he's going backwards or forwards in time, but it's safe to say that even on this glorious, sunny dawn of the new millennium, there's not a soul in the nearby town that wouldn't want to turn the clock back on the disaster of May 2000.

Just shy of Walkerton, the Saugeen drifts south to a meeting with Otter Creek as it loops back sharply almost due north and makes its way into the proud capital of Bruce County. The river is about fifty metres wide where it approaches the Highway 4 bridge to Hanover at the northeast corner of town. Generally placid in the winter, the Saugeen loses its calm in the spring. Fed by melting snow and seasonal rain, the icy water roars over the dam built years ago, often spilling into the low-level plain in the valley. Levels fall sharply in summer months, allowing the adventurous to walk along the concrete ledge below the dam all the way to a sluice cut out toward the far end. Near the sluice, outdoors enthusiasts have built a fish ladder so the salmon can bypass the dam. It wasn't that long ago that an eight-year-old boy slipped from the ledge and disappeared in the maelstrom below the sluice. It was left to Irwin Lobsinger, the town's former mayor and long-time volunteer firefighter, to come up with the old-fashioned way to find him. Lobie made up a bundle of blankets to approximate the boy's weight, attached it to a length of rope, and threw it into the water where he'd disappeared. When the bundle came to rest, Lobie rowed over and found the body, a cruel reminder that hidden in the life-sustaining water lurks an ever-present danger.

Once past the bridge, the river hugs the north edge of town as it flows westward, a high bluff to the north, a grassy, and treed plain to the south. Just past the second bridge, across from Lobie's Park and the old iron foundry, Silver Creek emerges from under a building and empties through an arched stone tunnel into the river. It was in April 1951 that the normally innocuous creek flooded amid torrential rain and mild weather, washing out three bridges in the process. In the 1960s, the flood-prone creek was rerouted upstream to spare the homes and yards that line its banks.

From its meeting point with Silver Creek, the Saugeen flows almost due north to Paisley and a rendezvous with the fast-flowing Teeswater River, whose waters have pushed north through the Greenock Swamp. The swamp is perhaps the single largest forested wetland in southern Ontario, although its vast, magnificent stands of old white pine are long gone. Huge canals dug by hand in the late 1800s provided logging access. For a quarter-century, millions of board-feet of white pine were taken, some finding its way to the fine furniture factories for which the area was once renowned. In the 1920s, with much of the logging heyday over, the labyrinthine canals in the inhospitable swamp proved to be an ideal hangout for bootleggers defying Prohibition. Still, even now, the wetland acts as a giant sponge for the Teeswater as it rushes to join the Saugeen, which presses onward past Port Elgin and onto Lake Huron hard by Southampton, 345 metres below the highlands from which it sprang.

Walkerton, one of dozens of small towns and hamlets that dot the landscape of Bruce County, owes its existence to the Saugeen. Its waters supplied the power needed for the saw- and gristmills that Joseph Walker built in the mid-1800s. But the large-scale logging and land clearing that came with the early settlers also left the town prone to flooding. Spring is the most dangerous time of year; a sudden mild spell, especially if compounded by heavy rain, can create a fast snowmelt. As far back as 1891, newspaper reports from Toronto, about two and a half hours and a world away, describe floodwaters washing out the bridge that gave the

town road access to the north. In March 1929, merchants and
shoppers on Durham Street, the town's main road that everyone
simply calls Main Street, found themselves trapped in their stores
as the Saugeen spilled its banks, sending waves of muddy brown
water gushing down the thoroughfare, and tearing up the recently
laid cement sidewalks. Boats ferried them out. A boy drowned
in the raging waters as he tried to cross the street to take a pair
of boots to his father stranded at the old station. They found his
body in a field. Record snowfall led to another severe flood in
1947, prompting the town to begin constructing a series of dikes.
Seven years later, those dikes saved the town from catastrophe.
It was in October 1954 that Hurricane Hazel swept north up the
Atlantic seaboard, causing devastation and loss of life in Toronto
before it blew itself out. On October 16, the Saugeen crested
almost 3.5 metres above normal. The lower end of town was
again under a metre of water, but there were no deaths.

Walkerton is not a whole lot larger than it was fifty or even one
hundred years ago. It is not a quaint town. It is a working town.
It is sturdy, not pretentious, like the tough-minded pioneers who
founded it. There is little that grabs a visitor's attention on a
casual drive through. Its charms, of which there are more than
a few, are mostly hidden. The area offers deer hunting in the fall,
and the summer Saugeen provides pleasant if not spectacular
canoeing. But it lacks the beach playground allure of a Port Elgin
or Kincardine – it is not a tourist town. The simultaneous arrival
of more than a few score overnight visitors taxes the capacity of
its three motels. Coming west from Hanover over the bridge
near the dam, Highway 4 runs into Durham Street. The small
stores that line the 250 paces or so of the main road are tidy and
utilitarian. The buildings, even the public ones, exude a human-
scale sensibility rather than an imperial folly. There is a sense of
history embedded in every street name, in the faded yellow brick
houses and weathered stone churches. There is a spaciousness
without sprawl: Walkerton is cradled on three sides by hills. Stores
and schools and churches and bars are all close at hand. A casual
dress code prevails. This is jeans and baseball cap territory. It's

the kind of town in which an unveiled bride, in full splendid regalia, can enter a packed bar at midnight on a Saturday and still have trouble catching the eye of the harried servers, perhaps even of the patrons who find it difficult to avoid stepping on her train. It is not a welcoming community, but it is a friendly one. The extended family, social, and church ties are strong. There are few visible minorities, yet there is a tolerance for diversity and a certain measured acceptance of eccentricity.

If Walkerton owes its existence to the Saugeen River, it owes its name to Joseph Walker, who arrived in May 1850 not far from what would one day become the Biesenthal farm to stake his first plot in the Queen's Bush. The vast swaths of untamed and unsevered territory had been home for ages to the Iroquois, Hurons, and Ojibwa. Settlement of the bush was encouraged, in part, to deal with the "Indian problem," and Walker was part of that pioneer wave. Described as short and squat, Old Joe as he became known was a miller raised in County Tyrone in Ireland and had connections to the Family Compact, the ruling elite of the pre-Canada province of Upper Canada. He'd spent time in the Toronto area before taking the plunge into Bruce County. When he clapped eyes on the small valley with its wild fruit trees and bush, Old Joe knew he'd found his spot. Armed with coveted mill rights obtained through his family connections, the forty-nine-year-old Walker set to work building a log cabin that would become the centre of his operations. He acquired ten farm lots in the valley. With the help of son William, he started the arduous task of clearing the trees for a sawmill he erected along the meandering Saugeen. He built a dam on the river for power, and had the mill machinery dragged in through the bush. By early 1852, Old Joe was in business. A year later, he borrowed $1,600 to build a gristmill, and again had the machinery dragged in through the bush. Walker also built several bridges over the river. One was ten kilometres upstream just outside Buck's Crossing, the settlement founded a few years earlier by Abraham Buck that would later become the town of Hanover.

Walker became reeve of the newly incorporated township of
Brant. By 1857, he started to subdivide his ten farm lots, giving
birth to a new town. The post office, which until then bore the
Brant township moniker, was changed to Walkerton. Undaunted
by the fact that it met none of the requirements, Old Joe set his
sight on having the fledgling town declared the capital of Bruce
County. When the Governor General granted him his wish that
same year, other towns, which felt more deserving of the honour,
howled in protest and the proclamation was set aside. A portrait
done about this time shows Old Joe smartly dressed in a bow tie,
his face framed by a mop of grey hair that covers his ears, some
of it spilling in curls onto his large forehead. A thick scraggly
beard hangs from his neck behind a clean-shaven chin. There's
a hint of defiance in his eyes. Along with his strong political
connections, he was after all one of the most prosperous businessmen in the county. Until the big crash of 1859. For several
years, municipalities and settlers alike had borrowed heavily to
buy property in hopes of big returns. But the buying spree drove
up prices to the point where railway expansion was no longer
viable. The speculative bubble burst. Municipalities found themselves strapped for cash or deep in debt, prompting the government
to shut down the Municipal Loan Fund on which they had drawn
so heavily. British investors began withdrawing. Then in 1858,
drought struck Bruce County, causing massive crop failure. Even
by pioneering standards, times were tough. The local newspaper
accepted firewood for payment. The county exchanged flour and
seed-grain for road work in an effort to stave off widespread star-
vation. The economic slump deepened with the turn of the decade
and the American Civil War. In an early example of the perils of
globalization, millions of people lost their jobs in England as
imports of cotton from the United States dried up and British
credit to the New World tightened further. There was no grist for
Old Joe's mill and little demand for the lumber that had once kept
his sawmill buzzing. Heavily leveraged, he went bust and was
forced to sell off his holdings at fire-sale prices. By 1863, he'd sold
almost everything, much of it to his influential friend, George
Jackson, the Crown land agent who had turned federal politician

and whose name still graces one of Walkerton's main streets. There are those who say Jackson merely took title of Walker's properties so they couldn't be seized and that he would later return them. In 1865, with Jackson's help, Walker at last won his crusade to have Walkerton designated the county town and he soon became its first mayor. But his days as tycoon were essentially over. Now approaching his seventies, Walker packed up in 1870 and headed north to Manitoulin, said to be the world's largest freshwater island. There he erected another gristmill. He died a couple of years later. The exact whereabouts of his grave are unknown.

In 1871, the settlement Walker had founded was finally declared a town by a special act of parliament. With just 995 residents, it didn't even meet the requirements for incorporation as a village. Still, the pioneers came, a hardy mix of mostly Irish, German, and Scottish settlers. Ever so slowly, Walkerton grew into a mini-hub for the farmers and loggers who braved the long, harsh winters and endured the short, hot summers. To the south and east, the province began its rush forward into the modern era, mostly ignoring the insular town and its hardscrabble inhabitants, who were more than happy to edge forward at their own quiet pace. Occasionally, big-city media did pay attention, such as when the *Globe* newspaper in Toronto reported on the floods of 1891. Toronto also watched closely in 1928 during a bitterly fought municipal election. The campaign pitted candidates in favour of getting the town's power from Ontario Hydro, the province's publicly owned electrical utility, against those who favoured staying with the local Walkerton Electric & Power Company. The company, which had begun supplying water-generated power for night use at the turn of the century, was the forerunner of the public utilities commission that Stan Koebel would one day run.

3

Just Another Well in the Swamp

Ⓢ TANLEY FRANCIS GEORGE KOEBEL was born March 23,
1953, into a staunch Roman Catholic family, the first of
nine children. Not the brightest of students, Stan was nevertheless conscientious, quiet, and serious, unlike his younger brother
Frank, who had a more impish streak and liked teasing his siblings. Frank would tell Stan made-up stories, then laugh at him
when he believed them. Their father, Frank Sr., had worked for
the town for years, becoming the well-regarded general foreman
of the works department. It was through his connections that the
nineteen-year-old Stan, who was battling his way through Sacred
Heart high school, secured a job as a general labourer with the
Walkerton Public Utilities Commission (PUC). Stan Koebel (pronounced cable) left Sacred Heart after Grade 11 in 1972 to begin
working full-time for the utilities commission. There were two
foremen at the time, one on the water side of the operation, the
other on the electricity side. Stan worked under both. Three
years after Stan started, seventeen-year-old Frank Jr. followed in
his footsteps, also joining the PUC as a general labourer. Frank

had just spent two months in Toronto training to be an auto mechanic when the PUC manager, Ian McLeod, asked him if he'd care to help out laying water mains. Frank accepted, soon becoming full-time. Stan eventually shifted over to the electrical side and became an apprentice lineman, passing his exams in 1980. It was the only formal training he had. Frank qualified as a lineman a few years later.

As the years tumbled by, young Stan impressed those around him with his work ethic, his willingness to do as told. He became known as someone who could be relied on to get the job done and get it done right. There was nothing slipshod about the way he worked. In fact, he was finicky, perhaps to a fault. McLeod never considered him the sharpest tool in the PUC shed, but Stan could cut deep enough, and that's what mattered. One morning in 1981, Stan arrived at work to find a white hard hat in his locker. He was now the sole foreman in charge of both water and hydro under a plan by McLeod to do away with the division between the two sides of the utility.

Although general manager, Ian McLeod was most comfortable out in the field with the boys, as he called them. He took an immediate shine to Frank, teaching him everything he knew about the water end of the operation. Perhaps it was the youngster's impish nature. Perhaps it was his stubborn, independent streak. Perhaps it was a certain common love of the bottle. But either way, Frank became McLeod's pet and the two men became fast friends. Where they might have disagreed was on the question of chlorination. Frank, who had grown up drinking raw water, didn't see much need for it. McLeod, however, insisted that his own family drink treated water. When he built a cottage in Sauble Beach in 1957, he ensured its well tested clean. Even then, well water was used only for cooking, bathing, or washing. Treated drinking water was kept in a forty-five-litre container on the kitchen counter. If they ran low, McLeod headed into town with the kids to fill jugs with treated water to take back to the cottage.

McLeod was a crusty fellow. He didn't much like being told what to do. After all his years on the job, perhaps he figured he

knew what he was doing and didn't much like any suggestions
to the contrary. He hated hearing complaints from townsfolk
about their tap water. In the early 1980s, the newly elected mayor,
postal worker Jim Bolden, discovered the manager's prickly side
at the first meeting he attended as a PUC member by virtue of his
position as top civic official. When Bolden tried to ask some
questions, McLeod exploded:

"No goddamn stamp-licker is going to come in and tell me
how to run the PUC!"

Bolden, who suspected McLeod had been drinking, was
dumbfounded. What angered him more was that no one else at
the meeting spoke up in his defence. Still, he soon developed a
grudging respect for the hard-working man who ran things his
way and ran them well.

Life under McLeod was pretty good all round. The girls in
the office liked him, although he didn't spend huge amounts of
time there. So did the boys. The daily routine had its diverting
moments, such as those provided by a gathering of "sidewalk
superintendents," those small-town old folk who can make a day
of watching young men dig a hole in the street and fix the water
mains below. Frank would pull the main and accidentally spray
them, somehow hitting them dead on every time. Then there was
the time Butch Kieffer got a job with the PUC and had to climb
a hydro pole. He froze in fear at the top and wouldn't, or couldn't,
come down. The other guys had to climb after him and throw a
rope over the cross-arm and tie it to him. Even then, they had to
pry the large man's hands and feet loose so they could lower him
to the ground. He didn't stay with the utility.

One day, PUC backhoe operator Don Herman received a distress call from his boss, whose truck was stuck out at one of the
town's wells. It was just before quitting time, but Hermy headed
out in his backhoe, where he extricated the vehicle. McLeod
retrieved a bottle of whisky and offered Hermy a drink, and the
two men shared a stiff one before heading home. Having alcohol
in the truck wasn't exactly proper, but as McLeod liked to say,
"Show me a man who never did anything wrong and I'll show
you a man who never did anything." Hermy didn't think much

of it. He was used to using his backhoe for unusual chores. One Boxing Day night, Hermy's highly pregnant wife said to him, "Maybe our child will be born tonight."

The snow was coming down heavily when the call came in: Hermy was needed to clear the roads. After promising to check in regularly to see how she was doing, he headed into the frigid night. He worked steadily as the snow fell, taking time out every thirty minutes or so to drop into the nearby police station to call home. At about four in the morning, she told him she could no longer wait. Hermy jumped back into his shiny John Deere loader and drove home, where he hoisted her suitcase and then his wife into the heated cab and drove her to the hospital a few blocks away. Having disposed of his passenger, he went right back to work.

"How's the wife?" a police officer asked when he got back about 5 A.M.

"She's up at the hospital," a triumphant Hermy replied.

"You're lying," the cop responded. "Your car hasn't moved. I passed there a few minutes ago and it's buried in snow."

Hermy chuckled. A short while later, his second boy was born safe and sound while dad tooled around in a backhoe, keeping the roads clear of snow. That's the way it was at the PUC. When needed, everyone worked long and hard getting the job done and then coasted a little the following day.

One summer, Herman began a Friday lunch ritual. He'd scoot over to the old Canada Spool and Bobbin factory on the other side of town and grab a bunch of turned hardwood bowling pins the factory had rejected. The other guys would stop by at the meat market and pick up a few steaks, while Hermy got a roaring barbecue fire going behind the PUC shop. The bowling pins made the finest coals. By 12:20 P.M., the feast began, accompanied by a beer or two from a twelve-pack one of the guys had stashed in the fridge, whose appliance whiteness stood out incongruously against the gloomy cement wall of the little room in the back corner of the shop. Ian McLeod always managed to show up just as they were tucking in.

"What are we eating today?" he'd ask wryly before joining them.

McLeod liked to be with the boys and he liked to share a drink with them, especially with Frank, who was developing his own serious problem with alcohol. But if the boss was partial to the bottle, he mostly kept it under control. It didn't seem to get in the way of his work although Stan said he had to drive him home one afternoon to sleep it off. Still, the town's lights stayed on and the water flowed.

In the 1930s, Walkerton drew its water from natural springs on the southwest side of town. Seven wells, dug about two metres across by three metres deep, tapped the springs to quench the town's thirst. So crystal clear was the water, you could see the bottom of the wells. The water naturally bubbled its way upward, overflowing into a large, open cement reservoir. (After one of Percy Pletsch's cows fell in and had to be hoisted back out, they covered the reservoir with chicken wire.) The slight elevation of the location allowed the water to flow naturally into town. For firefighting use, the town installed a huge steam-pump and boiler, which was constantly fired up just in case. When an alarm came in, the operator, who was always on standby, would turn on the pump, which was later replaced by an electric model. In July 1947, six people came down with typhoid fever. Suspicion fell on the drinking water. It wasn't the first time bad water had been blamed for illness in the town. In May 1902, people suspected the water in four cases of scarlet fever. The second time, however, samples were sent to Toronto for analysis. The tests turned up contamination. Doc Robbie Robinson, a local physician who had been practising in Walkerton since 1925 and had skis attached to the front of his car for winter driving, ordered all drinking water boiled before use. The municipality cleaned the reservoir and added chlorine to disinfect the water. It was time to start looking for a better source. In 1949, the town's first deep-drilled well was sunk, followed by Well 2 three years later. The springs were abandoned to spill their once precious cargo into nearby Silver Creek.

The new deep wells were good producers, but there was one major problem: the water was so hard, you could almost walk on it. Taps rusted out, toilet bowls and bathroom sinks stained an ugly yellowy-brown. Kettles had to be thrown out. Women complained of discoloured laundry. The water was also hazardous for infants because of its high level of nitrates, which can cause blue-baby syndrome, a condition in which the blood is deprived of oxygen. As a result, many homes used cisterns, tanks that collect soft rainwater, for washing or bathing. Others drew from their own wells for drinking. In the hot, dry summer of 1955, taps in the higher part of town ran dry. The recently formed PUC issued an urgent appeal for conservation. Watering lawns and gardens was banned. Kids' wading pools stood empty. It was obvious the town needed a more secure supply, so a third deep well was drilled in 1962, this one on the northwest of town. However, Well 3 was never a great producer and so, once again, the search began for a new source. The search might have ended with Well 4, which would've entailed tapping Otter Creek to the southeast of town. But enthusiasm for the site quickly waned when it was noted the creek was just downstream of Mildmay's sewage plant, and the well was never drilled.

According to the old adage, "You sink a well where there's water." Well 5 was sunk in 1978 near the old springs that once supplied the town, across the road from the PUC workshop. At last, the town had found a good source of soft water. Percy Pletsch, however, was none too pleased. Pletsch was a chiropractor. He also kept a small herd of Aberdeen Angus cattle and some ewes on a piece of land abutting the Biesenthal farm just outside town. The property on which he was born and raised had been in the family since the turn of the century. For water, they had always used their own well outside the farmhouse. Pletsch considered himself something of a connoisseur: he reckoned that his well gave the best-tasting water around. Pletsch was puzzled when, without any warning, a company showed up one morning and drilled Well 5 just outside his property fence. He figured it was crazy, given the low-lying ground on which it was situated. Just another well in the swamp, he thought. But puzzlement turned to upset when his own prized water lost its taste. He was disturbed enough to write Ontario's Ministry of the Environment. "The water tastes and smells like swamp water," he complained. Ministry officials came out and ran some tests. They did find that Well 5 was having a minor impact on Pletsch's well in terms of quantity, but dismissed his taste complaint. Nothing had changed in its quality, they said. Pletsch's palate begged to differ. As far as he was concerned, his water was no longer drinkable. But his complaints were the least of the PUC's problems. The utility had hired a consulting engineer for the development of the well, but manager Ian McLeod had given the go-ahead for its construction before the ministry had issued a permit. Despite their normally easygoing approach, this infraction struck the bureaucrats as direct defiance. They were furious. At an unusual meeting attended by the town mayor, senior ministry people reamed McLeod out. They even threatened the PUC with prosecution. McLeod was none too happy about the dressing down but, for once, kept quiet. Having made their point, the ministry officials proceeded to deal with their requirements for approving the well.

All groundwater, or water found underground, starts out with rain that percolates slowly downwards on its way to an aquifer, in essence a sub-surface stream. In the process, the soil and gravel above act as a marvellous biofilter, an efficient strainer of impurities and contaminants, such as bacteria. For that reason, deep-well water, the prevailing wisdom went, is as pure as it gets. Which is essentially true, unless the overburden, as the layer above the aquifer is known, is highly porous or very shallow or there are cracks in the rock that allow water from the surface to find its way directly into the below-ground channel. Then again, as far as deep-drilled wells go, Well 5 wasn't very deep. The limestone aquifer it tapped lay under bedrock covered only by about 2.5 metres of porous overburden. The water that fed the well flowed from two main veins at 5.5 and 6.5 metres below the surface. Not surprisingly, tests turned up signs of contamination, perhaps from the adjacent Pletsch farm. As a result, the ministry approved the well on condition that the water be properly disinfected and its quality closely monitored. It also recommended the town establish a protection zone around the well, perhaps by buying Pletsch's farm, to avoid agricultural or other pollution in the area. It also suggested the town keep searching for a better source of water, although it agreed Well 5 could act as an interim supply. The PUC accepted the conditions. A few months later, the ministry issued a permit, four days after the well had begun supplying the town with highly valued soft water. As was customary, none of the agreed-upon conditions were stated on the well's certificate of approval, which was filed someplace and quickly forgotten. Nor did the ministry do much to ensure the conditions were being met. Responsibility for vulnerable Well 5 was left entirely to the PUC. No one from the town ever did talk to Percy Pletsch about buying his land or otherwise limiting his farming activities. Within a couple of years, he sold the property and moved on, leaving the well he had once prized so highly to new owners. Although initially intended only as a stopgap, Well 5's soft water proved irresistible and it soon came to be seen as a permanent source.

In 1988, Ian McLeod prepared to retire. Stan Koebel, the foreman with a total of sixteen years experience under his belt, seemed the natural successor. McLeod, however, didn't think him up to the job. Don Herman wasn't too keen on the idea either. If anyone was going to take over, he figured, it should be Frank, the smarter of the brothers. Besides, Frank didn't like taking orders from anyone, least of all from Stan.

"Things are going to be different around here," Herman noted to his soon-to-be ex-boss one afternoon. "Could have one brother a manager, one brother a foreman."

McLeod looked at him.

"Don, it will never happen. Stan will never make a manager."

As always, McLeod had his own ideas. He lined up four out-of-town applicants and recommended them to the elected commissioners as the best candidates. Stan's name wasn't on the list. Even so, McLeod's qualified hopefuls never had a chance.

"Stan's a local boy," said the commissioners, who also happened to be good friends with Frank Sr.

"There's not anybody that knows as much about the Walkerton public utilities as Stan. He's worked here all his life. It's the only job he's ever had. Give him a chance."

There was another reason to want Stan in charge. Under McLeod, who himself hailed from Southampton, relations between the town's works department and the utilities commission were, at best, strained. The crusty manager simply didn't get on with his works counterpart, an equally obdurate German fellow who had been hired from out of town as an engineer. He'd try to tell McLeod what to do, but the stubborn utilities manager wouldn't listen. Things got so bad that the works department wouldn't tell the PUC before they dug up a street to lay a sewer or make other repairs. So a few months later, the commission boys would go out and dig up the newly repaired street to put in a water line. Kind of ludicrous, most folk agreed. That would all change if Stan took over. At least he and his dad got on, and his appointment would usher in a new era of cooperation between the works department and the utilities commission. It was a shoo-in. The commissioners interviewed Stan Koebel and, in their well-intentioned wisdom, decided to overlook his spectacular lack of formal qualifications or managerial experience. They did insist he take a front-line leadership course on handling employees. Stan took six management training sessions in far-away Toronto, then found himself at the helm of the Walkerton Public Utilities Commission. On his recommendation, his brother Frank succeeded him as foreman. McLeod had no say about either appointment. Don Herman shook his head but said nothing.

One of Ian McLeod's final acts as PUC manager was to officially open the town's newest well, Well 7. He sent out invitations to the mayor and councillors for July 26, 1988, asking them to the ribbon-cutting at the pumphouse, with refreshments at the Hartley House to follow. At the bottom of the notice were two words:

Souses welcome.

4

Good Intentions

$\mathbb{S}$TAN AND FRANK KOEBEL became certified waterworks operators without any formal training or testing. The Ministry of the Environment had begun implementing licensing in the late 1980s, and Ian McLeod had submitted the brothers' names under a grandfathering program just before he retired. Automatic certification soon followed. No one checked to see if Stan had the minimum Grade 12 education, as stated on his application. The brothers were similarly upgraded again in the mid-1990s when the growing Walkerton water system was reclassified. From time to time, Stan attended educational programs in the form of conferences put on by various waterworks associations. But, for a man of limited educational background and intellect, keeping up with changing rules and technology didn't come easily. Still, he was the boss. What was important to him was that the people around him considered him up to the job and that he didn't disappoint them. A large bookcase stood against one wall in his office at PUC headquarters. An impressive collection of files and literature stocked its shelves: association newsletters, pamphlets, textbooks, ministry rules, and requirements pertaining to the operation of a waterworks, chlorination bulletin 65-W-4.

He seldom read any of it. Even had he wanted to, it's doubtful he'd have understood much. Especially the government stuff, which often is written in the worst kind of dry, technical jargon. Nonetheless, Stan made up for his intellectual and technical shortfall with hard work and a demand for perfection. One time, he had a new summer hire trim a tree. The kid worked for the better part of a day trying to get it shaped just so and figured he'd done a great job. He called the boss on over to admire his handiwork.

"What do you think?" the youngster asked.

"It needs one more cut," Stan replied.

"Where?"

"About four inches above the ground."

If one of the guys hung a transformer on a pole and a wire wasn't bent just right, Stan would make him go back up and do it again. No matter how straight it seemed, Stan always demanded something be moved a little this way or a little that. That was the way it was: Stan gave the orders and that was it. It had to be done his way. But at least the hydro wires were as straight and as neat as any town could wish.

From his backyard, Mayor Jim Bolden watched as Stan oversaw the replacement of an aging hydro line that ran along the western edge of town. The line, owned by Ontario Hydro, was in terrible shape due to lack of maintenance. So the town bought it and, within two years, the PUC replaced it, poles and all, within budget. Another time, Stan oversaw the relocation of the unsightly hydro wires on Main Street to the alley behind the buildings. The project proceeded smoothly, with the cooperation of the various property owners, and, again, came in within budget. Stan obviously knew what he was doing.

Still, the promotion from foreman was tough for the rookie manager. It meant giving up the hands-on outside work he enjoyed and was good at in exchange for paperwork, office management, and overseeing the budgets. Running a hydro and water operation, supervising staff, and answering to town council are complex tasks, doubly so for a man with rudimentary management and accounting skills. In fact, the brains behind the financial side of the operation were those of Big Johnny Bell, the long-time treasurer of the commission who had a college education in accounting. It was left to Bell, who had an affinity for numbers and still did McLeod's income taxes on the side, to piece together the operating and capital budgets for the utility.

While the hydro side of the operation made money, the water side had always either run on a shoestring or lost money. If a main somewhere broke and needed replacing, crews simply used whatever material was at hand for the job. For years, no proper records were kept so that when pipes and sewers were put in the ground, the location was promptly forgotten. One time, some genius ran a water line inside the sewer line. When they dug up Main Street not so long ago to upgrade the water and sewer systems, crews found wooden catch basins no one knew were there. Other times, the mains weren't put in deep enough and would freeze solid in winter, leaving some residents without running water. To induce a thaw, PUC workers would run a current from the nearest hydro pole through the pipes, a dangerous practice that eventually became illegal. Walkerton winters were always a challenge for the boys, even if, mercifully, there hadn't been a repetition of February 9, 1934, when the town was noted as the coldest spot in Canada: -56°F. One particularly harsh winter, after the ploughs had cleared the roads, the frost penetrated deep into the ground and the pipes froze. The PUC responded by heading to stores in town and in neighbouring Hanover, where they bought up every available garden hose. They then connected the hoses from homes that still had running water to those that didn't. It was seat-of-the-pants, catch as catch can. But gradually, the PUC took a more professional approach.

To develop Well 7, the PUC borrowed $350,000. Other major upgrades to the water system were needed as well. That meant more borrowing. It didn't make much sense to John Bell to be paying interest to the bank, so he devised a scheme to self-finance by borrowing from the electricity side of the PUC. In that way, the hydro side would benefit from the interest payments. Bell also figured it would make sense to start putting money aside to build a reserve fund so future projects could be done without borrowing. Stan made the pitch to the commissioners. They thought it a great idea and approved it. Year by year, the reserve fund grew. The part-time commissioners – two elected officials and the mayor – were suitably impressed. The finances were in order, the utility was well run, and, perhaps most importantly, Walkerton had pretty well the cheapest water rates in the area. In the battle among small towns to lure new residents, business, and industry, cheap water is a major selling point. At one time in the early 1990s, Stan toyed with the idea of putting in usage meters as a way to generate revenue, which could then have been used to look for better water or to upgrade the system. Other towns were going that route both as a cash generator and as a conservation measure. The more it costs, the less people use, as they cut down on the waste that has made Canadians among the highest per capita users of fresh water in the world. The idea went nowhere. Stan figured massive rate increases or meters weren't wanted, so he never formally proposed them and no one offered. Instead, there were a few small rate hikes over the years that financed refurbishment of the town's two water towers and provided some money to upgrade parts of the distribution system. Walkerton residents continued to enjoy cut-rate water.

Managing a motley crew of outside workers also brought its challenges. Stan became more demanding. The two women in the office found him harder to get along with than his predecessor, and the atmosphere was often strained when he was around. Dealing with Frank, who along with a stubborn streak had never thought too highly of his big brother's abilities, was especially difficult. Over the years, Frank had developed a strong, hands-on familiarity with the job, and when it came to the water end of things, Stan seemed to rely heavily on his advice. Not only did Frank have the intellectual edge, he also had a natural touch with things mechanical. It didn't seem right to him that he should have to play second fiddle just because Stan was older and had arrived on the job a few years earlier. It especially bugged him when Stan,

who always began his days early, would show up at the PUC shop
first thing in the morning with a clipboard and pile of papers
looking, at least in Frank's mind, altogether too self-important.

"I can't work with my brother," he'd say to one of the other
guys.

Frank made up for being the number-two man by working
overtime, often taking home more money than Stan. Frank also
had a penchant for giving orders, evident even before he became
foreman. He brooked no challenge to his authority. Al Buckle
didn't seem to mind much. It was March 1992 when, in his late
forties, Buckle got a job with the PUC as a general labourer after
years in the construction business. He cut the grass, pulled weeds,
dug post-holes, and fixed water leaks. As Frank's helper, Buckle
did as he was told, and that was only as much as he needed to
know. He put up with his foreman's alcohol-induced irritability
on the job but shared friendly beers with him when the volunteer firefighters crossed the road from the fire station opposite
the municipal offices to Rob's Sports Bar and Roadhouse. At
work, sometimes Frank would tell him to get lost. Buckle did.
Sometimes Frank's speech would be slurred. Buckle took it in
stride. He didn't complain when he showed up at work dressed
in fairly good clothes only to have Frank order him into a muddy
trench he hadn't expected to be digging. At the wells, he watched
the way Frank did things and copied them. From time to time,
he was told to take chlorine measurements or fill out readings on
the log sheets, something he was not legally allowed to do. He
did as told. He said nothing when Stan or Frank changed the
numbers. Both were qualified operators and Buckle didn't ask
any questions. But it was nearing the end of the road for Don
Herman, who felt he could no longer please either brother. Little
more than a year after Buckle joined the PUC gang, Hermy
slipped into retirement, a little bitter at the way the brothers had
treated him in his final years.

Frank's love of the bottle was compounded by increasingly
complex health problems. A borderline diabetic, Frank's blood
pressure was consistently too high. He began putting on serious
excess weight, though it didn't show that much on his bull-like

frame. The first clear sign of how bad it was getting was a mild
heart attack in January 1997. But he returned to the job and the
drinking continued. Stan did his best to discourage it, even
sending him home one day to sober up. In early 1998, Frank had
a second minor heart attack, after which he spent more than a
month at a rehabilitation centre. At the shop, Stan laid down the
law: there would be no more beer in the fridge, no more drinking
on the job. Not that the boys used to run around drunk all the
time. Not when there were high-tension wires to handle or poles
to climb, a job to get done. On special occasions, though, such as
birthdays or anniversaries, it wasn't unusual to knock off early and
have a couple to celebrate. The arrival of out-of-town road or other
construction crews also offered an occasion to chug back a few at
one of the local motels, and Stan participated over discussions
about the projects. This is, after all, a hard-drinking county. But
Frank's illness had cast a new light on things. Stan decided there
would be no more drinking during any part of the workday, not
even on special occasions. Frank would be coming back and
there'd be no temptation. Frank did seem much better when he
returned from drying out. The boys were busy with water-main
reconstruction on Main Street, and he immersed himself in work
with renewed vigour. For a while, at least, things appeared to be
humming along.

Days after Frank was felled by his second heart attack, Stan
received another piece of unwelcome news: a Ministry of
Environment inspector would be coming down from Owen
Sound as part of the government's waterworks inspection
program. It was only the third time in more than a decade that
the ministry had formally inspected the town's facilities, the
first time in three years. Previous inspections had turned up
numerous deficiencies, including the presence of potentially
dangerous E. coli bacteria in the water and a lack of proper
testing and training. The ministry had written Stan, making it
clear that the presence of E. coli indicated unsafe water. Each
time, he promised to do better, but bad results kept turning up,
dozens of times over the years. Stan didn't relish the prospect of

an inspection. Ministry people made him nervous. Seemed like there was never a familiar face from one contact to the next. He was pleasantly surprised when a friendly, relatively young woman showed up a week later and introduced herself.

In the male-dominated world of environmental officers, Michelle Zillinger was something of an anomaly. Zillinger had already spent eleven years in the business in various locations around the province when she joined what was essentially an old boys' club at the Environment Ministry's local office in Owen Sound in the fall of 1997. She was given the task of inspecting area water and sewage works, and Walkerton's number came up in February 1998. Checking the records, Zillinger noticed E. coli had consistently shown up over the past three years. She immediately concluded there was a problem with the way the PUC was disinfecting.

Adding chlorine or a chlorine compound is an established method of getting rid of bacteria in water. As it dissolves, hypochlorous acid is produced. It's highly effective, as long as the acid has the fifteen minutes or so it needs to work its way through the outer membrane of the bacterium and cripple its ability to reproduce. Tracking the amount of chlorine in drinking water subject to bacterial contamination is therefore crucial. It's especially critical when its source is a vulnerable well, such as Well 5 was, a fact explicitly noted and discussed during its construction in 1978, a fact promptly forgotten by everyone.

A pile of government guidelines laid out the various requirements for chlorination and monitoring, although few people, even those ministry officials charged with overseeing compliance, seemed familiar with them. Ian McLeod never did have much use for red tape. Still, he figured it was best to keep the government officials happy. In 1980, the ministry had written him to praise his excellent monitoring of the water quality and for his chlorine records. Had they looked more closely at the daily operating sheets for Well 5, they might have noticed that all the chlorine numbers looked suspiciously similar. McLeod and his protégés seemed to find it simplest to fill in the log sheets with columns of identical numbers reflecting the ideal values the ministry people wanted to see. Heck, it made them happy, and that meant they stayed off the manager's back. The water, coming as it did from a deep well, was good. Everyone knew that. In fact, many a small town didn't bother adding any chlorine at all. Besides, people in Walkerton were pretty quick to let McLeod know they didn't much care for the taste and smell of chlorine. A couple of times, the PUC even flushed the system to lower the levels of the chemical after a barrage of complaints. Frank, too, hated the taste of chlorine in the water. As far as he was concerned, the less the better.

In preparation for the inspection, Stan went out to the wells to spruce them up. He looked over the log sheets that Al Buckle had been filling out in Frank's absence. On several occasions, Buckle had not made it out to the wells and had simply marked the column for chlorine residual with a dash. That wouldn't do, Stan decided. But he worried perfect numbers might raise suspicion. So under his careful hand, what had started life out as dashes became 0.4s, not quite the recommended chlorine level, but close enough.

During her visit, Michelle Zillinger made it clear to Stan that the number of bad test results he was getting was unacceptable. Stan mentioned how residents complained about the chlorine. Zillinger was sympathetic. She knew that to be a common complaint. She asked Stan to produce the monthly log sheets from the well. He showed her the February sheets, which he had finessed. So while the numbers appeared to reflect reality, the reality was the amount of chlorine in the system fell short of the guidelines. Zillinger didn't ask to see the sheets from previous months. No one had ever told her she should. But had she done so, she, too, might have noticed that the February logs were an anomaly. The others all showed perfect, unvarying chlorine dosages and readings day after day, even though in any normal system, the amount of chlorine used can vary widely, even by the hour.

Zillinger was troubled by what she saw. She stressed the importance of chlorination. Stan said he'd do better and promised to start a proper sampling program immediately. He listened attentively as she walked him through the various requirements.

She explained proper record maintenance. She also pointed out he hadn't kept any logs under rules that required operators of waterworks to have at least forty hours of training a year. Stan didn't mention that no one was getting much training. It's not like there was any money or time for it. Still, he was grateful for her personal attention and detailed advice, the first a ministry person had ever provided him. He noted her visit down as six hours of training on a handwritten log he immediately began keeping.

While other municipalities were also failing to meet the guidelines, Zillinger was particularly worried by what she found in Walkerton. There had been so little improvement since the previous inspection three years earlier, so many of the same problems. Given the potential danger of pumping contaminated water to the town's taps, she decided that a reliance on Koebel's promise to do better, no matter how sincerely made, just didn't cut it. It was time for legal action. Zillinger wrote up her report and recommended issuing a legally binding order to the PUC. It didn't happen. The culture that infused the Owen Sound office amounted to an unwillingness to rock the boat. Asking for voluntary compliance with the guidelines had been for years the ministry's preferred method of dealing with problem waterworks. The Conservative government of Premier Mike Harris, with its pro-business approach and antipathy toward red tape, had made it abundantly clear that aggressive enforcement and prosecutions would not be the order of the day. Besides, the government's severe downsizing of the ministry had effectively hobbled its ability to police environmental violations. And so, despite the strong and well-considered views of the woman who had joined his staff in the ministry's Owen Sound office just a few months earlier, supervisor Phil Bye overruled any direct action. The situation didn't seem too bad, Bye said. There were indications that Stan Koebel was trying to make improvements. Instead, Bye recommended sending a stern warning letter threatening legal action if Stan failed to take appropriate measures. Zillinger realized there was no point pressing her case. She drafted a letter pointing out the many deficiencies with the Walkerton water system along with a warning that legal action would follow if they weren't promptly addressed. Compliance, the letter warned, would be "closely monitored" over the next several months. Koebel, as manager, was given sixty days to respond. The letter, along with Zillinger's detailed inspection report, went out in May 1998 under Bye's signature. Copies of both the letter and report were sent to the area's public-health unit, the municipality, and Stan's elected bosses at the PUC.

That the commissioners had Zillinger's report and the letter threatening legal action put Stan on the spot. Not that the people he answered to understood much of the technical mumbo-jumbo. None had read the Ontario Drinking Water Objectives, the guidelines under which waterworks operated. They weren't required to and no one had ever suggested they undertake the task. Like most elected commissioners in small towns everywhere, they had no expertise in the area of water. Nor were there huge numbers of qualified people clamouring to become a part-time commissioner, not even for the $500 or so they were paid every three months. Most who stood for office were civic-minded citizens who were acclaimed election after election, sometimes only leaving their posts when they died. It was after one such death that Jim Kieffer, whose brother had once got stuck up a pole, moved up to become chairman. It wasn't their job to ask questions about the day-to-day operations. That's what the manager was for: to ensure whatever needed doing was done, to let them know if there were any problems. Ian McLeod had liked it that way, and so did Stan Koebel, who assured them the little matter with the ministry was well in hand. He told them he'd talked things over with the helpful inspector and had set up a new sampling system. He also announced he'd started a training log as the ministry had demanded. The commissioners took him at his word. There was no reason not to. That unpronounceable *Escherichia coli* that had been detected didn't mean much to them. It sure didn't have the ring of something that could kill anyone, not to them, not even to most of the ministry people for that matter. Whatever it was, Stan would take care of it. Just as reassuringly, the ministry had said in its letter it would be monitoring the situation closely.

In fact, the only monitoring the ministry did was to await Koebel's response. It came in July 1998, two weeks after the sixty-day deadline had passed. His letter suggested he was doing his best to meet their concerns. "We will be up to the minimum sampling program by the end of July," he wrote, a clear sign he was still violating the testing guidelines five months after Michelle Zillinger had visited. He also promised to maintain the recommended amounts of chlorine in the system and even held out the idea of installing special equipment to ensure that happened automatically. Yet even as he penned his letter, Stan knew the chlorine levels were once again too low. Zillinger had convinced him that proper disinfection was more than just red tape strung out by an indifferent bureaucracy. Frank, though, remained unpersuaded. Stan would boost the levels to as close to ministry guidelines as he dared, and Frank would immediately lower them to a level he deemed acceptable. Given that Frank was the foreman who visited the wells regularly, Stan didn't have much chance of winning the bizarre chlorine tug-of-war. He tried talking to his younger brother about it, to no avail. Frank's almost religious faith in the quality of the water was not for the shaking.

Testing chlorine levels at the wells was Frank's job; Stan looked after monitoring the distribution system. Usually, that meant taking a sample at his home or office. As long as he found some chlorine, he was happy. Stan knew that the numbers Frank wrote down on the wells' daily log sheets were bogus, but no one at the ministry ever looked closely at them. Using Frank's figures, he carefully did the math to compute the monthly averages and sent them to the ministry to meet its request for annual updates. He worried about submitting reports he knew were phony. He needn't have. A year after Zillinger's visit, Stan received a letter from the Environment Ministry's Owen Sound office.

"The ministry conducted an inspection of your facility on February 5, 1998," it stated. "There has been a noticeable improvement in the operations of your waterworks since that time. I thank you for your efforts and cooperation in this regard."

Stan passed the letter onto the commissioners. He had dodged another bullet. Although Michelle Zillinger remained of the opinion that stronger action had been called for, the local ministry office was officially delighted by Stan's response. He was obviously well intentioned. Then again, it is also true that the road to hell is paved with good intentions.

Michelle Zillinger's February 1998 inspection report had also landed in the laps of town councillors, and at least one of them found it alarming. Mary Robinson-Ramsay had gone into local politics after watching short-sighted councillors almost succeed in committing the historic town hall to the wrecker's ball. Robinson-Ramsay was an unusual councillor in other ways. Although she'd lived and taught in Walkerton for twenty years, she was born in Toronto, raised in rural Ontario in neighbouring Grey County, and had gone to high school in Switzerland. Her grandfather was one of the first medical officers of health in Ontario. Her physician father was also a medical officer of health. In addition to attaining a music degree from the University of Toronto, she'd spent time in rural South Africa, where serious water-borne diseases, especially in rural areas, are not uncommon. She knew Zillinger's report spelled trouble.

"Fortunately at this time, there were no major problems as a result," she wrote in a note she prepared for a council meeting. "Probably oversight rather than deliberate neglect."

Even if looking after the town's water supply was the PUC's responsibility, Robinson-Ramsay realized that it fell ultimately under the municipality's jurisdiction. A *Toronto Star* newspaper report on the problems created by the Conservative government's decision to get out of the water-testing business only served to underscore her concerns. The article noted that the ministry had singled out twenty-three municipalities for substandard testing of their drinking water. To Robinson-Ramsay, this proved the importance of having the provincial government act as a watchdog. But the government was going in the exact opposite direction.

"We have worked too hard for too many years to create good public health to allow it to degenerate due to neglect," she wrote.

She suggested council think about hiring a qualified public works manager to oversee both water and sewage. She argued that the increasingly complex management of water required regular and ongoing technical expertise. But her fellow councillors, who didn't seem to grasp her concerns about bacteria, decided against any action. What's more, they had only been elected for a one-year transition term because the town was set to merge with two neighbouring townships in light of municipal amalgamations the Tory government was demanding. They felt that any decision was best left to the council of the new municipality, due to take office six months later. There was no urgency anyway. The PUC, under Stan's diligent leadership, was taking care of any problems and the ministry had said it would be watching closely. Councillors argued further that the report had been sent to the medical officer of health, Dr. Murray McQuigge. He would no doubt act if he thought it necessary. What they didn't know was that McQuigge figured the ministry was taking care of matters and would let him know if there were problems. Still, Robinson-Ramsay did manage to get council to accept her proposal to ask Premier Mike Harris to ensure the Ministry of the Environment remained responsible for water quality. They also asked that the premier take another look at how smaller municipalities were coping with the various other responsibilities the province was thrusting upon them. Harris's response didn't amount to much.

"Thank you for writing to inform me of council's resolutions regarding the realignment of provincial municipal services," Harris wrote. "I have noted council's views and appreciate being kept informed of its activities."

Ramsey-Robinson didn't run in the ensuing election in which Dave Thomson, who lived out of town, came to office. The Zillinger report was soon forgotten, a mere blip in the consciousness of the municipality. At the public health unit office in Walkerton, it was filed away, essentially unread. Stan Koebel was again left to his own devices. But Koebel's tough juggling act was getting tougher. Johnny Bell, who had been an invaluably steady hand on the tiller of the PUC's finances as secretary-treasurer, went home one evening and had a massive heart attack.

Bell's death left a huge hole in the PUC office. The silver lining for Stan was that it didn't take too long to find a replacement in the form of Janice Hallahan, clerk-treasurer in nearby Neustadt (One of Canada's Prettiest Villages, the sign says), birthplace of former prime minister John Diefenbaker. Conscientious and personable, Hallahan exuded confidence and competence. Her background in business administration and accounting and varied experience in municipal finances made her ideally suited for her new job, which she tackled with enthusiasm. In Hallahan, who was born and raised in Walkerton, Koebel found a managerial soulmate on whom he could lean as heavily as he ever had on her predecessor.

At the beginning of 1999, the PUC's reserve fund for the water system was a healthy $449,401. This was money that could be used for system upgrades and maintenance on Well 5, on which virtually no work had been done in almost twenty years. Of its three working wells, Well 7, the newest, was the one on which the town relied most heavily. It produced more than enough good quality water. The one problem was its balky chlorinator. Flush with cash, Koebel ordered two replacements, one each for Wells 6 and 7. The new units were compatible with an automatic chlorine residual analyser, which Stan hoped to add on at some point. The device tracks chlorine and shuts a well down automatically if levels fall too low either due to mechanical failure or an upsurge in contamination. That would preclude the hassle of the constant manual checks that fell to Frank and his helper Al Buckle, who mostly relied on weigh scales that had never worked properly and a bubble in the chlorinators to judge chlorine dosage. Having duplicate equipment would also make repairs and replacing parts smoother. It would be efficient, modern, and safe, just like the ministry wanted. Stan asked Frank to take care of installing the new chlorinators when they arrived. Frank had other things to do.

At about the same time, the Tory government in Toronto, forever looking to downsize, made a far-reaching decision that would create more problems for Stan: it announced plans to break up the century-old monopoly enjoyed by the publicly owned Ontario Hydro and deregulate the electricity market. What Bill 35 essentially meant was that utilities such as the one Stan ran would be forced to go out onto the open market to buy power. Utilities were given less than two years to figure out what they wanted to do. They could sell to Hydro One, one of Ontario Hydro's successor companies, or form cooperatives or amalgamate with other area utilities to form large enough outfits to compete. Walkerton's PUC hooked up with a group of other small-town operators to search for the best way to face the brave new world of deregulated electricity. There were endless meetings, many of them out of town, and Stan found himself away from the office and his regular work. Until this point, Stan had been spending as much as 20 per cent of his time managing the town's water. But the introduction of Bill 35 saw that allotment of time plunge drastically. From then on, he was able to spend mere minutes a day on water. The legislation also created waves of uncertainty for the town and PUC in general, for Stan in particular. What would happen to the water operations if the PUC had to divest itself of the hydro side? Perhaps the municipality would take over the water itself. Maybe the PUC could continue running the water only. Perhaps an outside agency could come in. What would it all mean for the PUC staff? What would it mean for him? The ground under Stan Koebel's feet was starting to feel like quicksand.

5

Labour Pains

B OB MCKAY was the new guy in the PUC shop, having joined the utility only in May 1998. He hadn't planned on going into the world of high-voltage electricity. The family farm in the Woodstock area seemed like a better bet. But a tornado roared through in the mid-1980s, throwing their new thirty-metre silo onto the barn. With skyrocketing interest rates and not enough insurance, the family was forced to sell. McKay, who'd studied field-cropping and livestock management at college, did some odd jobs before landing a position with the nearby Norwich utilities commission. For the next ten years, he worked both in Norwich and then much farther afield in eastern Ontario as a qualified lineman. When a job opened up in Walkerton, he jumped at the chance to move with his wife and four children so they could be closer to family. Ministry inspector Michelle Zillinger had recommended to Stan that he consider hiring another qualified waterworks operator. With Frank off recovering from his heart attack and another outside worker, Tim Hawkins, in hospital, the suggestion made sense. Stan, backed up by Zillinger's recommendation, had no trouble persuading the commissioners to go along with the idea. It was, after all, the first time he'd ever indicated that he needed extra help. At his interview, McKay asked about advancement prospects. Stan said there weren't any. What Stan didn't say was that he was hiring him to replace Hawkins, who had suffered a series of crippling strokes a few months earlier and was unable to walk. It appeared he would never be back to work, or so Stan thought after visiting him in the hospital and seeing the rough shape he was in. Had McKay known the job might be temporary, he would never have accepted, but he settled in quickly. Stan was good to him and McKay considered him the best boss he'd ever had. If they worked through their lunch hour, Stan would often buy them something to eat. Frank, though, was far less friendly, even downright standoffish. Perhaps he felt threatened by the rookie's solid grasp of the basics of water management that Bob had gained at his previous jobs. He also had a waterworks operator licence into which, like Stan and Frank, he'd been grandfathered. Actually, Bob figured Stan had hired him because he needed another certified water operator, but for months Frank wouldn't even show him the wells. McKay finally insisted, and Frank grudgingly took him out but wouldn't say a word when they got there. It seemed the foreman just didn't want him around. It didn't matter much anyway. McKay spent almost all his time working on the hydro side.

Five months after he started, McKay had too much to drink on the Labour Day long weekend and was charged with impaired driving in Woodstock. Given his probation had a month to run, he figured he was in deep trouble. There was no way around it: it was either quit or be fired. Dejected and afraid, he walked across the road to Stan's home on Yonge Street on the holiday Monday and offered his resignation. To his astonishment, Stan was having none of it.

"Don't worry about it, it could happen to anybody," Stan said. "We'll work through it."

"Well, I'll accept anything the commissioners say," McKay stammered.

"They pretty much back what I want," Stan responded confidently.

Stan did knock him down in pay, but that seemed fair. Stan also asked McKay to accept an extension of his probation by one year, the expected length of his driving ban. Glad to have kept his job, he signed the paper Stan presented to him. McKay mentioned what he'd done to Steve Lorley, a fellow PUC lineman who acted as the union steward for the outside workers. Lorley thought it crazy that McKay had agreed to the probation extension because it made him vulnerable to layoff at a whim. Lorley put on his union hat and persuaded Stan to tear up the letter. Stan reluctantly agreed, but McKay's good relationship with his boss got torn in the process.

"Your licence suspension has given the utility undue hardship," Stan told a startled McKay one day.

That wasn't true. Two or three of the guys usually did the hydro work together so it made little difference if one couldn't drive.

Stan's initial kindness to the probationary employee he could have fired on the spot was coming back to haunt him, and the ghost was Tim Hawkins. Far from being down for the count, the quiet, lumbering utility worker with a gentle face had made something of a miraculous recovery from his strokes and wanted back to the job he'd done for seventeen years. Stan, who had obtained permission to hire McKay on the premise Hawkins would never return, found himself up a pole without a ladder. Having Hawkins back would mean one person too many on the payroll, but letting his recent hire go, someone who'd moved his wife and four kids to Walkerton, didn't seem right either. He decided to fight: Hawkins would represent a danger to himself and the public because of the mild lingering paralysis in one of his hands and leg. The commissioners accepted Stan's view. The disappointed employee turned to the union, setting off a long, nasty labour battle. In a grievance filed in February 1999, the union argued that the PUC had a duty under human-rights legislation to take Hawkins back given that he'd been medically cleared to return. Stan turned the matter over to a lawyer. The atmosphere in the shop began to deteriorate, although Frank seemed to side with his brother on this one.

In October 1999, Steve Lorley called a meeting with Stan over the stalemate. Lorley, too, had had his moments with the boss. Although he'd taken it in stride when the youthful Lorley had also been charged for impaired driving and lost his licence, Stan didn't much like his union involvement.

"For every little thing, you go to the fucking union. Why are you going to the fucking union?" he said once.

Another time, Lorley was about ten minutes late for work.

"Sorry about being late," he said.

"How come sorry cuts it with you when you are shoving this union bullshit down my throat," Stan snapped before sending him home on the spot.

Lorley grieved and the suspension was undone. In all, the union filed ten grievances over a period of seven years through the 1990s. Invariably, Stan backed down and the grievances went away. His commissioner bosses had little inkling that things at the shop were anything other than hunky-dory. But Stan was showing no signs of backtracking when it came to Hawkins. At the meeting with Lorley, Stan dug in his heels. A month later, Lorley called in reinforcements in the form of a union staff representative, who brought along a doctor, a physiotherapist, and someone from the insurance company. They met Stan and the PUC lawyer at the Walkerton public library on November 11, briefly halting the discussions at 11:11 A.M. to observe Remembrance Day. By the end of the meeting, Stan knew he couldn't win. Still steamed, he took it out on Bob McKay a few days later. It was six weeks before Christmas.

"Tim's coming back on a six-week trial," Stan told him. "If he makes it, you're gone."

"I just want to work," McKay pleaded.

"Well, we won't need you."

Greg Diebold, another PUC hydro worker, overheard the exchange. He moseyed over and told Stan he might be leaving soon and there would be no need to lay McKay off.

"It makes no difference," an irate Stan insisted, turning back to McKay. "In six weeks you'll be gone."

It had been barely eighteen months since McKay had moved his family to Walkerton. He had no desire to search for work again. Feeling afraid and vulnerable, he turned to the union, which sent Stan an angry letter. The PUC lawyer responded immediately.

"Mr. Koebel is willing to admit he lost his temper during this exchange," the lawyer wrote. "However, he apologizes for any hurt feelings."

Hawkins' return was now a *fait accompli*, but resentment among the outside workers festered. Stan's resentment lingered as well. When Hawkins began a trial work period to prove he was fit for the job, Stan ordered him to climb a hydro pole, something he would normally never have needed to do. Hawkins struggled up.

"See, Bob. He can't climb. He won't be able to do the work," Frank observed.

It was embarrassing, but Hawkins made it. Stan then told him to raise the heavy wooden cross-arm a metre. Hawkins managed to drill a hole for the arm's new location but, because of the weakness in his leg, couldn't climb and carry the load as well. It was senseless, vindictive. Hawkins clambered down in frustration, leaving the cross-arm in place. Stan watched, then spun on his heels and left. That Christmas, the two secretaries in the office along with McKay, Lorley, and Hawkins boycotted the PUC Christmas party. No one wanted to eat and drink with the man who'd fought so hard to keep Hawkins out, then treated him so badly on his return.

On January 1, 1999, the sprawling three-ward municipality of Brockton was born, its name a compression reflecting the unwieldy alliance of Walkerton with the predominantly rural townships of Greenock, to the west, and Brant, which surrounds the town. The provincial government's policy of amalgamation was designed to increase efficiency: it made no sense to have several councils with their myriad councillors, reeves, and mayors, when one larger unit with fewer politicians would do. Watching the name given their town by Joseph Walker 140 years earlier become a suffix in the new municipality was one slightly bitter pill to swallow for Walkerton residents. Harder to swallow was that each of the three municipal wards had two councillors, leaving the town with one-third representation despite having half the population of the new municipality. Although it has just about five thousand residents, Walkerton is nevertheless something of an urban metropolis in comparison to its new, rural partners. And for the first time, its mayor, Dave Thomson, wasn't a resident of the town. Walkerton and Brant, in particular, had a long history of petty conflict. Any expansion by the town meant encroaching on the township, which resisted fiercely to preserve its tax-assessment base. The Walkerton public cemetery remains in Brant cheek by jowl with cornfields after a failed attempt at annexation. So does Mother Teresa elementary school, although it is one of the rare exceptions in that the town supplies it with water. It might have made a whole lot more sense for Walkerton to join forces with its slightly larger urban neighbour and rival, Hanover, ten kilometres to the east. That option was never considered. Hanover, which always seemed a little more prosperous, maybe even holier-than-thou, is across the border in Grey County. In their zeal to reform and modernize the hodgepodge system of municipal government, the Tories in Toronto seemed to have overlooked the system of county governments devised 150 years earlier.

The amalgamation also brought two smaller communal wells into the PUC fold. Both were given much needed but time-consuming upgrades and attention. Still, Frank and Al finally set about replacing the chlorinators for the town's own wells. They started with Well 6, even though it was just the backup. The job began on Groundhog Day, February 2, 1999. Although it should have taken about three days, it ended up taking several weeks, meaning that whenever the well ran, as it did on numerous occasions, it did so without any chlorinator at all. Frank didn't think it mattered much. Stan figured it was no big deal either. As long as one of the other wells pumped chlorinated water, that would be enough to keep the system safe. In any event, Stan had less and less time to worry about chlorine levels. Preparing for mandatory hydro deregulation kept him hopping. He worried increasingly what impact the separation of the hydro and water would have on his career and on the jobs of his underlings. At the very least, he figured, the PUC should retain responsibility for the water, perhaps with Frank in charge, even if the electricity side was spun off to a new entity. That would allow the independently minded utility to continue its proud tradition of more than forty years as stewards of the town's water. Besides, no one knew the system better than he and Frank.

In the fall of 1999, the municipality began turning its mind to its water operation. Mayor Dave Thomson asked for suggestions. It was time for Stan to make a pitch. He provided Janice Hallahan with a bunch of printed material and asked her to put together a proposal extolling the virtues of the PUC. Hallahan worked her magic, producing a document entitled "A Day in the Life of a Drip" that proudly proclaimed, "Brockton water tastes great!" Replete with cartoon characters of water drops, the proposal highlighted the advantages of a PUC-run system. It noted numerous tasks carried out by PUC staff, among them sampling for chlorine residuals daily and documenting well readings. It stressed how sample results were sent to the manager and the Environment Ministry, which in turn would immediately report anything unusual to the manager, who would then act promptly to resolve any problems.

"Retaining the water services with the PUC would provide assurance that the operation of the utility would remain with public accountability," the proposal went on. "Should the municipality transfer the water services back into the works department, the municipal staff would not possess the same 49 years of extensive familiarity and knowledge that collectively the current manager and foreman have with the water distribution system."

Hallahan, of course, had no idea just how close to fantasy this document was. Nor did council. In October 1999, the town agreed the service should remain with the PUC. Stan had won the

battle. The war was far from over. Some councillors still wanted
to dissolve the PUC and have the works department take over the
water. Also, the hydro situation remained in flux. There were still
decisions to be made and approvals needed from the provincial
government. It all seemed to be taking forever and the uncertainty weighed heavily on Stan. Moreover, the tensions with his
staff lingered, and the ministry was again making half-hearted
noises about bad results. But trying to get Frank to see the
problem as serious was a non-starter. The second chlorination
unit, the one meant to replace the balky one at Well 7, the town's
main supply, had been sitting for a year in a box at the pumphouse. Frank and Al never seemed to find the time to get it
installed. Stan, meanwhile, was just about at the end of his tether.

Stan had always been a busy guy. In 1992, his wife of sixteen
years left him. She complained he was always working and there
never seemed to be enough time for family and vacations. Not
only was he managing the PUC full-time for which he earned a
decent $52,000 a year, he also moonlighted as an electrician for
friends and neighbours. If there was a job to be done, Stan did
it. He'd also do stints as a bartender at the local arena and served,
as did Frank and Al Buckle, as a member of the town's volunteer
firefighting unit. The family split along gender lines, with Mary
taking their fifteen-year-old daughter, Stephanie, while twelve-
year-old Jacob chose to stay with Stan. He sold off the family
home and divided their assets, for which he paid Mary $38,425.
But the acrimonious divorce would also create lasting financial
pressure. Along with $250 a month he paid for Stephanie's
ongoing support, he also ended up with a ten-year obligation to
pay his ex-wife $900 a month in spousal support.

Stan's domestic waters calmed with his eventual remarriage
to Carole, although it did mean having to disavow the Roman
Catholic Church of his immediate family. At Trinity Lutheran, a
short walk down the road from their home on Yonge Street, Stan
and Carole found a safe religious refuge. But his life in the secular
world felt more and more like a Wall Street rat race. On top of
everything else, he and Carole took over the cleaning contract at

the PUC offices, arriving at the crack of dawn a couple of times a week to clean the place. Perhaps he was reacting to the uncertainties of his future job prospects by trying to run harder. Perhaps he figured he could impress the new mayor and council with both his diligence and competence. Perhaps he was simply trying to run from his own self-doubts. He began to feel as if he was sinking. And he was.

6

Gathering Clouds

THE NEW MILLENNIUM brought little respite for Stan Koebel. There were several major construction and maintenance projects set to go, but Greg Diebold had quit, Al Buckle was on sick leave with carpal tunnel syndrome, and Bob McKay had hurt his knee. Tim Hawkins was back, but Stan continued to harbour doubts about his ability to function as lineman. Topping it all, council was still dithering about what to do with the waterworks, although it now seemed to be leaning away from leaving them with the PUC. Without telling Stan, council retained a consulting engineer. It also started billing customers directly for certain charges, again without telling him. Stan felt left out of the loop, as if he were losing control, and the persistent spring rains weren't helping his mood.

"I'm supposed to be in charge," he complained to Carole. "It doesn't seem fair they're billing the customers for the water and collecting money the PUC needs."

He made the same complaint to the PUC chairman, but there didn't seem much Jim Kieffer could do other than advise Stan to hang in there. Council, ultimately, was in charge and would make the decision. So Stan ran harder, from hydro meeting to hydro meeting, from project to project. And still events conspired to catch him off guard. One such event was the decision by the private laboratory that had long tested Walkerton's water to get out of the business.

GAP EnviroMicrobial Services had come into being after its owner fell victim to the axe wielded by the Conservative government. For twenty-six years, Gary Palmateer had worked in the ministry labs that did the water testing before the province decided to shut them down in 1996 and turn the system over to the private sector. In Walkerton's case, that made for a relatively smooth transition because GAP knew exactly what was required. Although the reporting guidelines were never updated to reflect the privatization of the laboratories – much to the consternation of senior Environment and Health Ministry officials – Palmateer nevertheless followed the rules that had applied to the public labs. Whenever he came across bad water samples from Walkerton, which he did on a dozen occasions, he notified the PUC as well as the ministry office in Owen Sound, which in turn was supposed to let the medical officer of health know. But the lab to which Stan Koebel turned when GAP closed in spring 2000 had no such history. Although A&L Canada Laboratories East, a U.S.-based franchise operation, had never tested for bacteria and was not accredited to do so, it nevertheless accepted water samples from Walkerton. In the absence of updated guidelines or regulations the provincial government felt no need to implement, A&L followed private industry practice in deeming test results to be confidential, to be shared only with the client. It certainly never occurred to Stan to discuss the notification protocol with A&L in the event bad water turned up. He simply assumed the company would tell the ministry, as GAP had always done. As recently as April 2000, after GAP passed bad results on to them, Larry Struthers of the Environment Ministry's Owen Sound office spoke to Stan about the problem, but he neither followed up nor passed along the information to the medical officer of health.

A day after the unsettling phone call from Struthers, the PUC auditor raised the issue that Stan had racked up 99.5 unused vacation days. The credits had been accumulating over the previous decade, but had really shot up over the last few years. Although entitled to six weeks holidays a year, Stan typically took only one or two. What with the meetings and trying to attend various courses or conferences, he felt guilty about taking off again. He never did get to take that vacation.

If a well sits idle for too long, the volume of water it yields can decrease. So Stan took the town's main well out of service and fired up Wells 5 and 6 to ensure their aquifers stayed open and clean. But he also had another reason to run Well 5, which had been put in service in 1979 as a temporary source. Unlike Wells 6 and 7, which were farther out of town and on a different power grid, Well 5 used PUC-supplied power. That meant it generated revenue for the utility as it pumped water. Stan figured that was pretty smart. He left it that way for eight weeks until May 2, when he changed the computer-operated cycle to put Well 7 back in service as the primary well, with Well 5 and then 6 kicking in as backups in that sequence. Stan was anxious for Frank to get the new chlorinator installed at Well 7. The old one had really been acting up, and the new one had been sitting in its box at the pumphouse now for almost eighteen months, "partly installed" is how he put it in his monthly manager's reports to the utilities commissioners.

"It'd be nice to get 'er in," he said to Frank yet again.

Early on the morning of May 3, 2000, Frank sent Al Buckle and Bob McKay out to Well 7 and told them to wait for him. Around 7:40 A.M., Frank arrived and told them to take the chlorinator out. Frank pulled the main disconnect to the power supply for the pump and Buckle proceeded to hacksaw through one of the plastic pipes. Within a few hours, they had taken the chlorinator, but not the well, out of service. Given that the installation should only have taken a few days, neither brother considered it much of a problem that the town's main well was pumping raw water.

April had been a wet month, with heavy rain on the 20 and 21. But the rainy weather had given way to more than a week of glorious sunshine and unseasonably high temperatures, affording farmers a great opportunity to get onto the land. Across the fence from Well 5, Dave Biesenthal had taken advantage of the perfect days to spread the manure that had been accumulating over the winter from his cow-calf operation on the fields, plough it into the ground, and get his corn planted. In and around town, bare legs and arms emerged from a winter of hibernation, as coats and sweaters drifted toward the back of closets. Mothers pushed their strollers at a leisurely pace, kids on bicycles took to the streets, and students sat on benches and munched their doughnuts as they caught a few rays. Everywhere, people greeted one another with "Beautiful day, eh?" All seemed right in the world. Although still technically weeks away, it felt as if summer had already arrived. The light showers that had fallen May 1 before giving way to another week of warm, sunny days only added to the mood of optimism in both country and town. Even Stan Koebel was feeling a little better about life, busy as it was. He'd sent off the weekly Monday samples to the new lab, and although A&L had some funny ideas about how to fill out the submission sheets and the amount of water they needed to do the tests he wanted, it didn't seem like anything that couldn't be sorted out later. After all, the old lab had always known what to do. Stan was also looking forward to a waterworks association conference in Windsor. While it would take him away from Walkerton, it would also be a respite from the day-to-day pressures. Janice would take care of the office. Frank could look after the outside work, especially the big water main construction project out by the corner of Highways 4 and 9 on the south end of town. But the great weather couldn't last.

The early-morning rain was heavy on Monday, May 8, when Stan reached Frank at the shop.

"How are things going? With the highway job?" he asked.

"They haven't got good sample results yet," Frank replied. "Oh yeah. I didn't want to tell you this over the phone, but Steve lost his licence again, got picked up by the cops . . . for impaired." "Well, I guess we'll have to deal with it when I get home." "Yeah, and Bob's going in for knee surgery tomorrow." That took Stan by surprise. He knew McKay had twisted his knee climbing a snow-covered slope at work in January, causing a pop that made both Lorley and Hawkins take notice. Although he'd hurt it again a month later, it seemed to be doing better, and Stan had been under the impression McKay's therapy was working. Oh, well. Frank could figure it all out. But Frank was having trouble figuring it out. He hadn't gotten around to installing the new chlorinator at Well 7, which had been pumping raw water into the system now for five days. In the wee hours of the next morning, Well 7 shut down altogether. Well 5, with its long history of bacterial contamination, took over. Well 6, with its relatively new chlorinator, didn't kick in, possibly due to a lightning strike. Throughout the town's water system, chlorine levels fell lower and lower. With Stan away, and so much else to do, no one was paying much attention.

At the waterworks conference in Windsor that day, rookie Environment Minister Dan Newman delivered a glowing report on the state of Ontario's water. He made no mention of the billions of dollars needed to upgrade the province's ailing water and sewage system. He did not mention the deep budget and staffing cuts to his ministry or the confusion created by the hasty dismantling of the public laboratories that used to test municipal water. He didn't mention the problems the changes had created as to how bad results were reported or the fact his ministry knew many small towns were not treating or testing their water properly to save money. He did not mention that several senior officials in his ministry had been sounding the alarm for years.

"Ontario's drinking water is second to none," he boasted from the podium, adding that the PUC managers were to be congratulated for delivering "safe, reliable water."

The PUC managers weren't buying. After Newman left, they passed a resolution demanding the province return to its role as guardian of the province's water, not unlike the one Walkerton's council had passed two years earlier and sent to Premier Mike Harris, to no avail.

At A&L labs, the weekly samples taken that Monday arrived from Walkerton. Robert Deakin wasn't happy. The labels on the bottles didn't match the submission forms, which was on GAP letterhead. Nor had they sent enough water, an issue Deakin had discussed with Stan. He called the PUC, only to be told the manager was away. When he insisted on talking to the next guy in charge, Frank called him back. Deakin tried to explain the problems: there were no samples from Well 5, the forms weren't filled in properly, and they hadn't sent enough water. Frank didn't have a clue what he was on about.

"Just proceed with what you have," he said.

Outside, the rain continued to fall, as it did almost non-stop for the rest of the workweek. But on the Friday night, the violent collision of atmospheric warm and cold fronts spawned savage thunderstorms and it really began to pour. At the local arena, Frank helped out with a night of well-attended fun in which the town's volunteer firefighters put on a show impersonating the Backstreet Boys and Spice Girls, much to the delight of the families and kids. But lightning made the hydro foreman in him antsy. He left early and drove around for a spell to see if there'd been any damage. It didn't seem like there was and he went on home. His wife was at work and the kids were still out, so he watched some TV, then hit the hay. He was soon oblivious to what meteorologists would come to describe as a "60-year rainfall."

PART TWO

THE DELUGE

7

Night of the Storm

Friday, May 12, and Saturday, May 13, 2000

THE BROOD MARE was ready to foal. Dr. David Biesenthal donned his boots and made his way to the front field to see whether she was ready to accept a helping hand. The rain, which had been coming down fitfully if heavily through much of the evening, was really pelting down. Lightning split the night sky as if angry gods were venting their fury on a hapless world. Biesenthal headed back inside. It was way too late anyway.

"To hell with you, you're going to have to do it alone," he said to his mare through the driving rain. But there was no trace of animosity in his voice.

The following morning, runoff had washed into the family room. Outside, Dave's wife, Carolyn, noticed a strong mouldy smell, especially in the far corner of the farm by the highway. It smelled like dew worms. The rain gauge showed the storm had brought fifty millimetres of rain in a matter of hours. In the wet front field, a newborn foal struggled uncertainly to his legs, his mother nuzzling him in concerned encouragement. Night of the Storm, with his glossy brown coat and dazzling white patch on his forehead, had become the latest family member born on the Biesenthal farm.

Biesenthal was also relieved to find the storm has caused little damage. His care in tilling and planting his crops had paid off. There was no standing water and no evidence of serious runoff from the fields. He and Carolyn had bought their fifty-hectare farm and moved there from their house in Walkerton in 1973. He'd been working in a general veterinary clinic he and a partner had founded on the road to Hanover. But the farm, just minutes from the southwest edge of Walkerton, proved an ideal spot for a small cow-calf operation, cash cropping, and a horse clinic. Standing at the top of the long drive in front of the clinic and looking out over the fields of corn or beans, it's easy to imagine being miles from urban civilization. Yet the nearest Becker's convenience store is just minutes away. The entire farm, including the cozy two-storey yellow-brick L-shaped home with its small, well-tended flower garden in front, bespeaks a quiet pride. There is no debris or junk or any of the other bric-a-brac often found on rural properties. On a perfect May afternoon, with the magnolia bush flowering in full pinky-purply glory, it's as close to an idyllic spot as anywhere.

In front of the barn, lowing calves were finding their legs, oblivious to the man watching them. There was a bit of scrub on the far side of the newly sown field about 150 metres to the east of where Dave Biesenthal stood. He'd driven past that bit of bush a thousand times over the years but never realized that what lay behind it was Well 5, one of the wells that fed the nearby town with drinking water. He had no idea, of course, that the recent rains, especially the big Friday-night storm, had pushed a lethal bacterial predator down beneath the emerging crops and fertile soil into the aquifer that fed the well that was being pumped to the taps of the town.

In Shallow Lake, about an hour's drive from Walkerton, Mayor Dave Thomson was getting edgy as the Friday-evening agricultural meeting wound down. He could hear the fierce storm and it reminded him of one back in the summer of 1977, when lightning set his barn on fire.

"We'd better get out of here and get home," he said to his wife, Helen.

The rain pelted the windshield as they drove. Huge drops seemed to dance above the road as they bounced off the glistening blacktop. The Thomsons were almost home when they noticed the lights gleaming off the inundated fields.

"Holy, we must have had one terrible rain down here," Dave said.

The river that runs through the Thomson farm had flooded. On Saturday morning, he could see his cows over at the far side of the field, where they had sought higher ground, although they were still standing in water. Spring flooding isn't unusual, but not since Hurricane Hazel in 1954, when four calves drowned, had the farm looked like this. Thomson and his son grabbed the tractor, hitched the wagon, and dumped a couple of bales of feed onto it, hoping to drive across the flooded creek and lure the cows back over toward the barn. Only the top strand of the page fence showed above the water and the wagon actually floated as they hauled it across. But it was for naught. The cows weren't going to follow the wagon for any amount of feed. By Mother's Day Sunday, the entire fence was submerged. It would be another day before the top page peeked through the muddy water again.

Mother's Day, Sunday, May 14

Compared to the storm of 1947 or even that of Hurricane Hazel in 1954, the damage caused by the vicious Friday-night downpour was relatively minor. Some of the town's low-lying streets flooded when the Saugeen spilled its banks. Half-a-dozen cars were partially submerged and some tree branches were down, but the skies had cleared and the cleanup was underway. Mother's Day Sunday saw families and friends get together or head out for a meal. Some townsfolk engaged in the old ritual of walking out onto the bridge by Lobie's Park, where the water had reached the first or second rung of the children's slide, to watch the rushing river below. Word on the street was that the river would crest sometime in the early afternoon. The small island just to the east was almost submerged as the waters rose to within a metre of the bridge. On the west side, Silver Creek flowed furiously into the Saugeen. It was a fine day for river-watching or for celebrating an anniversary, as provincial police Const. Jamie McDonald and his wife, Cathy, were doing. Jamie took his children to one of the parks to marvel at the flooding. In Hanover, Peter Raymond and his physician wife, Esther, packed little Mary Rose into the family car and headed west to Walkerton to celebrate their second Mother's Day at a restaurant. Small-town life. Small-town pleasures. Small-town peace.

The first Stan Koebel knew of the storm came as he drove down the steep Highway 4 dip and over the bridge into town by the Tim Hortons on his way home from his week away. As he passed the old Canada Spool and Bobbin smokestack, standing like a forlorn relic from another age in an otherwise empty field, the Saugeen struck him as unusually high, as if from a fast snowmelt. That didn't make much sense though, given the unseasonably warm weather of recent weeks and the fact that the April rains had already washed away the snow.

Monday, May 15

As was his custom, Stan Koebel was up early for the start of the new workweek. He headed to PUC headquarters with Carole to clean and start catching up after his time away. There would be lots to do. He checked the computer system in the office that ran the town's wells. Well 7 was flashing "fail," signifying a power interruption. Assuming that Frank had replaced the chlorinator, Stan turned the well on from the office. It would be several hours before Well 5 would shut off automatically. On his desk, he found a stack of papers, including faxes from A&L labs. One set indicated what the laboratory needed for the microbiological testing of Walkerton's water. Robert Deakin had spoken to both Stan and Frank about this but decided to spell it out in writing. Stan shoved the fax aside. A second fax, however, caught his eye. This one was dated May 5, the Friday before he'd gone away. Perhaps it had arrived while he was out of the office. Perhaps he'd just been too busy to pay it any attention. The report contained the results of the weekly samples taken May 1. Bacteria, although not E. coli, had been found in both the raw and treated water from Well 5. Results were similar for samples taken at the PUC shop and office. Stan wasn't worried. The tests merely indicated the water quality was getting worse. All that was needed was some extra chlorine and the next set of tests would come up just fine. That's the way it always went. He headed over to the PUC shop, where he told Steve Lorley he was going to haul him before the commissioners over the impaired driving charge. Stan looked decidedly unhappy. Al Buckle came in.

"Big storm must have knocked out the power to Well 6," Buckle told him.

"What about 7?" Stan asked.

"We didn't get the chlorinator in. Been too busy with the con-tractors."

Stan frowned. That meant Well 7, which he'd just turned on, was running without any chlorine. Frank arrived.

"Mind if I have the day off being that I worked Saturday?" Frank asked.

What could he say? Frank and Bob McKay had spent most of their Saturday at the high school repairing the electrical equip-ment damaged by flooding from the big storm. The chlorinator would have to wait. There was too much else to take care of.

"Yeah, go ahead," Stan said as he headed out. "Just get Al to sample Well 7 before you leave."

That Al Buckle was, in the words of Larry Struthers of the ministry, qualified only to wash the floors wasn't on anyone's minds. Although he couldn't legally do the weekly sampling because he had no licence, he'd been pressed into service whenever Stan or Frank couldn't do it themselves. Frank had shown him the ropes and Buckle was pretty good at following instructions. It was also pretty easy to smooth over any problems with the log sheets. Then again, Frank didn't care much for the whole sampling rigmarole anyhow. Over the years, he'd developed his own system and passed it on to Buckle, who asked no questions, and Stan had gone along with it. At one point, Frank used to go down and take a sample at the store at 125 Durham Street, until it changed owners and became a supermarket. Regular sampling day for the PUC was Monday, and staff at the store would be busy at the sinks washing and preparing vegetables for the post-weekend shelves. In his mind, Frank felt he was getting a couple of hairy eyeballs when he walked in and told them to "shut 'er down for a couple of minutes" so he could take samples. He didn't need the aggravation. So he stopped going there but continued labelling the sample bottles, which he filled elsewhere, as having come from that address. Often, he would just go the tap at the PUC shop, fill a bottle, and label it as having come from some other place in town, such as the municipal office, where no one ever sampled, or the supermarket. It sure saved time and hassle. What did it matter anyway? Water is water is water, Frank figured. No one would ever know where the samples had come from, certainly not the lab. Stan, however, would usually grab a sample at home, perhaps at his mother-in-law's place if he happened to be in the neighbourhood, or, most conveniently, from a tap at the PUC office. The same approach was taken to checking chlorine residuals. Often, Frank or Buckle would simply check a small bead in the chlorinator that indicated whether chlorine was moving into the system. Frank told Buckle that he could tell how much chlorine was in the water by "checking the bubble." Buckle believed him. Absolutely. Buckle checked the bubble diligently. As far as Frank was concerned, doing everything exactly by the book wasted time no one had. Gradually, the PUC monitoring system became less and less reliable, but no one seemed to notice and no one seemed to be hurt by it.

Frank called Buckle over. Because Stan had said to sample at Well 7, he figured Well 5 was shut down so there was no need to bother with it.

"Go sample at 7," Frank said.

"But 7 ain't running," Buckle responded, not realizing that Stan had just turned the well on.

"Stan says it is. So that's the place to take samples."

"You sure?"

"Look. Mind your own business and just do what you're told. Now take the samples and hurry up and get back. I'm outta here."

Frank went home. He, too, didn't worry that the town's main well was running without a chlorinator and would continue to do so for four more days. Heck. The water was good.

Stan drove around the corner to check on the big pipeline construction project on Highway 9. The job site was a mess. The pit holes, excavated areas where the mains were being laid, were full of water from the big storm and needed cleaning out. The project was running behind schedule and the contractor was anxious to get things moving. A missed deadline would cost the company money. Stan was eager to help, to show he could get things done. He agreed to the contractor's request to send samples from the new main to the lab along with the PUC's regular Monday samples of the town's system. He called Al Buckle to bring over some test bottles. Buckle soon arrived with them, along with the samples he'd just taken at Well 7. They filled the empty bottles with water from the new main and Stan took the lot back to the PUC office, where he quickly filled out the submission forms.

"Please rush. Thanks, Stan," he wrote on the sheet for the samples from the new mains.

Tuesday, May 16
10 A.M.

The package provoked consternation at A&L labs the next morning. This wasn't the way they'd explained the samples had to be submitted. Cathy Doyle, the lab's assistant supervisor, called Stan. She explained they needed more water to do the proper testing. Stan seemed to be preoccupied.

"Do you have the results for the rush samples from the new main?" he asked.

"We just got them not fifteen minutes ago," she protested.

"Well, we need them."

Doyle relayed the conversation to her boss, Robert Deakin. They just don't seem to get it, Deakin thought as he headed to the phone.

"It's too soon to see any kind of result," he explained to Stan. "We need a minimum of twenty-four hours."

"Could you rush the samples anyway?" Stan asked.

"If something comes up, within twenty-four hours, we'll let you know."

Deakin asked why there were no samples from Well 5, which had shown bacteria from the May 1 testing two weeks earlier.

"It wasn't running," Stan replied. "But we need the rush ones done. We're trying to get something up and running."

Around Walkerton, people were starting to feel poorly. The flu was doing the rounds. Or so everyone thought.

Wednesday, May 17
8:30 A.M.

The lab technician called Robert Deakin over. Walkerton's water was obviously contaminated. Deakin took a look himself. The samples from the construction site had all tested positive for bacteria, including E. coli. He checked the other samples. Raw water taken from Well 7 tested clean, but, strangely, the treated water from the well was showing serious contamination. The water from the town's taps, including a sample labelled as having come from Stan's house at 902 Yonge Street, showed similar problems.

"Better get a report to them right away," Deakin said. "I'll try to call them."

"The samples for the main have failed," Deakin told Stan. "The other samples don't look good either."

The second comment didn't register with Stan, who was thinking about the bad samples from the Highway 9 construction site. He was wondering why they had failed. He barely paid attention as Deakin ran through a detailed list of the bad results.

"How many?" Stan asked when Deakin had finished.

The question struck Deakin as odd.

"Well, we did a membrane filtration test on one sample and the plate is covered with both coliform and E. coli bacteria. I haven't had a chance to count how many yet, but it's high. I'll fax the report as soon as I can."

"Okay, thanks," Stan told him.

Late that morning, A&L faxed the results of the water-main tests to the PUC. A couple of hours later, they sent the other results, the ones showing serious contamination in the town's drinking water. In the interim, Stan found Frank to let him know that the samples from Highway 9 had come back positive. He made no mention of Deakin's warning about the others.

"We're going to be reflushing, but we've got to send four more samples right away," he told Frank. "We won't be able to start up service until we get good results."

Frank wasn't worried. Although he'd never seen it before, he'd heard somewhere that mains often fail their first test, that it's not unusual to find bacteria in new pipes. Even a discarded doughnut can cause problems. Besides, the main wasn't on line yet. Flushing and rechlorinating would fix the problem. Stan passed on the same information to Al Buckle and asked him to collect four samples from the mains to be sent to the laboratory right away. At the construction site, he ran into the site supervisor, who asked to see the bad test results.

The two men headed back to the PUC office. The faxed results from the new main were on Stan's desk. He gave the supervisor a copy. On the desk, the other sample results, the ones showing gross contamination of the drinking water, lay unheeded. Around town, doctors were starting to take calls about illness, diarrhea, nausea. Stan was running around, checking on other projects and preparing a report for the PUC commissioners' meeting the next evening. There was always so much to do.

Thursday, May 18

Bob McKay turned up late Thursday morning at the PUC shop to let Frank know the knee surgery he'd had a week earlier had gone well. He'd be seeing the doctor at the end of the month and would have a better idea then of when, exactly, he'd be able to get back to work.

"How's the money doing?" Frank asked, trying to be friendly.

As they chatted, Frank mentioned the construction on the Highway 9 water main.

"How's that going?" McKay asked

"Not well. They had bad test results."

"Not good."

"Yeah. That's going to set 'em back until they get 'em re-sampled."

That Frank had even in passing mentioned the bad samples struck McKay as odd. Frank had never really warmed up to him and the two men had never talked much about the water.

"Oh yeah, Stan wants to see you," Frank said as McKay prepared to leave.

After lunch, the construction contractors asked Frank about hooking up the fifteen-centimetre line from the Highway 9 water main to Saugeen Filter Supply, the farm supply outfit that took over the site after the Canadian Tire store closed. The store planned a grand opening for the coming long weekend and wanted to be able to clean up the front of the property. They also needed water for fire protection. No one would be drinking it, they assured him. Stan wasn't around, so Frank decided to give the go-ahead, even though the mains hadn't yet tested clean.

"Just make sure you leave the water running inside the building so there's no chance of back-feed into our system," he said.

He then headed out to Well 7 with Al Buckle to finish the job they'd started two weeks earlier: installing the new chlorinator, which had been in a box at the pumphouse for almost a year and a half. They began mounting the equipment on the wall, installing the scales, and lifting the tank onto them. There were several plumbing connections to make, and the motor on the booster pump, which had been overhauled, needed rewiring.

At the PUC office, Stan was agitated. He made it clear he was unhappy that McKay wanted to put his knee through workers' compensation insurance so that he wouldn't have to use up his sick days.

"I'm getting tired of everybody," he told McKay. "No one wants to do anything."

McKay was taken aback. The outside crew took their orders from Frank and always did as told. He wondered why Stan was telling him this instead of his brother, but McKay bit his tongue. Stan wasn't done.

"Steve will only be with us for another two weeks if he loses his licence," Stan said in reference to Lorley's having run afoul of drunk driving laws for a second time.

Janice Hallahan, who watched the exchange from her office adjoining Stan's and found it upsetting, decided to take an early lunch. McKay soon followed her out the front door as Stan turned back to preparing for the evening's monthly meeting of the PUC commissioners. Besides dealing with the Lorley issue, he also needed to provide his regular monthly manager's updates. He sorted through the papers on his desk, glancing at the laboratory reports showing the contaminated water. He slid the A&L faxes under a pile of papers. There was more than enough other stuff to tell them:

- PUC staff changed a forty-foot pole on McGivern Street beside the hospital. The old pole was rotten at the ground level.
- Changed over three-phase line and transformer at the Welcome to Walkerton sign at the south end of town.
- Highway 9 water project: pressure tested great, now waiting for water samples to come back, then we can start changing over the services.

- Disconnected hydro and water service to 105 Durham Street, the building has been torn down.
- Connected two underground hydro services in Snider subdivision.
- Relocated three-phase meter service outside for Granny's Restaurant at the customer's request.
- Connected one new underground hydro service in Fisher subdivision.
- Currently rebuilding the chlorine equipment at our seventh pumphouse.
- Flooding on the weekend caused some damage to the primary equipment at the WDSS.
- Disconnected 4 Yonge Street North for the weekend. Water was up to the main floor.
- Sewage plant's three-phase service was changed over to the new equipment on May 17.
- Disconnected hydro and water at 15 Orange. The home was damaged by fire.
- Contractor has started the water and sewer project on the old Durham Road and OH borrowed a 25 KVA transformer from us on May 14, 2000.

That evening, the commissioners, including Mayor Dave Thomson, accepted Stan's report without discussion. They teased Chairman Jim Kieffer about his twenty-fifth wedding anniversary, which he planned to celebrate on the long weekend. Outside, Bob McKay waited in his car. He'd driven a worried Steve Lorley to face the music before the commission. Stan had already made it clear Lorley would likely be fired.

"How'd it go?" McKay asked when Lorley emerged.

"I still have my job," Lorley smiled.

In Hanover, two-and-a-half-year-old Mary Rose Raymond was running a fever and suffering from diarrhea. Her mom, the family doctor, was not yet terribly worried. Neither was Tracey Hammell too concerned as Kody began exhibiting similar symptoms at home in Walkerton.

8

It Can't Be the Water

Thursday, May 18
9:30 A.M.

THE LITTLE GUY was in pain. His swollen tummy ached. Bob Panabaker, the child's family doctor in Hanover, suspected appendicitis. Because the nine-year-old was diabetic, Panabaker decided to refer him to a pediatrician rather than directly to a surgeon. Only two full-time pediatricians work in the region, Kristen Hallett and Ewan Porter, whose offices are located in a converted three-storey house in the western corner of Owen Sound about forty-five minutes to the north. Hallett, who was on call, took the referral, and the boy's parents drove him up to the Owen Sound hospital. The noon hour normally provides some much needed downtime for Hallett, a chance to eat a pasta lunch brought from home and heated in the microwave, but instead she drove over to meet her newest patient.

Trim, fit, and possessed of a winning smile that exudes confidence without arrogance, the energetic Hallett hadn't planned to be a pediatrician. She was from the St. Catharines area in southern Ontario and had graduated as a pharmacist. But two years in the business left her wanting more. She pondered earning a doctorate with the idea of becoming a clinical pharmacist in a big hospital but opted instead for medical school. The refreshing ways of children and the complexities of treating their illnesses led her into pediatrics. Helping sick kids would provide the challenges she sought, but not in a big city, where the plethora of sub-specialties would limit the opportunity to apply everything she'd learned. Finding work in a smaller centre close to home proved impossible and she grew tired of looking. When she heard of an opening in Owen Sound, much farther from St. Catharines than she would have liked, she initially balked. She gave in finally, and moved there in July 1999 at the age of thirty-one.

Hallett examined the boy in the hospital and quickly ruled out appendicitis. She put him on an IV to control his diabetes and settled him in bed to wait and watch. That evening, he developed bloody diarrhea, at just about the same time as a second young patient, this one a girl, arrived at the hospital.

"I don't think I've referred anyone to you before," Panabaker said to Hallett. "And now I've sent you two in one day."

Nor is it an everyday event that patients arrive with bloody diarrhea. To have two at the same time is rare, even in big-city hospitals, and pretty well unheard of in Owen Sound. Hallett found seven-year-old Aleasha Reich in the emergency department. Examining her was difficult because they could barely get her out of the washroom. Aleasha had come home from Mother Teresa elementary school in Walkerton with stomach troubles two days earlier. Her older sister, Amanda, developed a fever and cramps the same night. On the Thursday morning, Cathy Reich phoned the school again to let them know her kids wouldn't be in, and the secretary mentioned that about twenty kids were sick. When Aleasha developed bloody diarrhea and started throwing up, Cathy took her to the emergency department in Hanover, where her family doctor practises. The hospital initially suspected a virus and sent them home with instructions to drink lots of fluids. By the evening, she was much worse. This time, Aleasha saw Panabaker. He suggested Cathy drive her to see Hallett right away. Like the boy now resting on the ward upstairs, Aleasha didn't complain much, miserable as she was. Adults complain much more, Hallett thought.

There are half-a-dozen infectious causes of such symptoms, and the doctor, not long out of her pediatric residency, still knew them by rote: salmonella, shigella, campylobacter, E. coli . . . The symptoms, however, pointed most squarely in the direction of E. coli O157. Besides, Hallett had seen one case before, not six months earlier.

Little more than a century ago, not too many years after Joseph Walker first gazed upon the valley that would become home to Walkerton, a renowned German pediatrician and micro-biologist named Theodor von Escherich identified the bacteria found by the billions in intestines of humans and other mammals. In his honour, *Escherichia coli* were named. Newborn babies, emerging as they do from a sterile environment, only come into contact with E. coli after birth. Within days, the hardy bacteria, which live with or without oxygen essentially feeding off whatever they find, colonize the infant gut. There they live, multiply every twenty minutes or so, and die – a cycle that repeats itself for as long as their new host survives. For anyone who cares to count, a gram of human feces might turn up about 100 million of these bacteria. Among the most primitive of all life forms, E. coli are normally benign. In fact, they are essential to our well-being, helping us to synthesize certain beneficial vitamins. But bacteria are susceptible to bugs themselves, killer viruses that invade their delicate plasmic skins, where they multiply until the host bacterium explodes like an overblown balloon. Somewhere, sometime in the past, just such a virus infected an E. coli bacterium, but instead of killing it, the invader left behind its unwelcome signature: genetic instructions on how to produce the potent poison known as verotoxin or Shiga toxin. A mutant killer bacterium was born.

A visitor turning off Durham Street with its rows of tidy stores soon finds himself on quiet, tree-lined streets flanked by bungalows and two-storey homes interspersed by almost stately yellow-brick houses that date to the Victorian era. There is scant evidence here of the 1980s building rush that saw subdivisions of identical houses mushroom in and around the sprawling cities and towns of southern Ontario. Still, there is little in this pleasant, residential area that gives away the fact that this is just a good-sized village. An easily missed dot on a map, where people know their neighbours and their neighbours' kids, who deliver newspapers from wagons they pull behind them. Only the occasional whiff of freshly strewn manure wafting over from the farms surrounding the town or a tractor or combine rolling down the main street pegs this as an agricultural area.

Provincial police Const. Jamie McDonald and his wife, Cathy, a fellow officer he'd met on the force, moved from their rural home in 1997 to take up residence next door to Bob McKay. The move was intended to broaden the social horizons of their two small children, escape the hassles of caring for a septic tank and private well, and be real close to work at the police detachment in Walkerton. From their yard, the McDonalds often saw Stan Koebel cutting the grass in his own small backyard across the street. It was a perfect spot and the couple planned to spend the rest of their days there.

Thursday, May 18
6:30 P.M.

Jamie McDonald headed down to the drugstore to get some medicine for three-year-old Kylie, who had come down with a nasty bout of diarrhea.

"Oh, your kids have it too?" remarked pharmacist Ken Brown. "They are just dropping like flies all over town."

Kylie's five-year-old brother, Ian, would soon be suffering the same affliction.

Thursday, May 18
8:30 P.M.

While young Aleasha Reich was stuck in the washroom, Dr. Kristen Hallett chatted with her mom in the hallway as she tried to puzzle out the cause of the illness. She asked what school the girl attended, then called from emergency to the ward nurse to have her find out where the boy, admitted earlier, was from. Both, it turned out, were from Walkerton. Both were students at Mother Teresa, although in different grades and they didn't know each other. Given that E. coli O157 is usually food-borne, Hallett quizzed Cathy Reich about what her kid might have eaten. Had there been some kind of potluck dinner, a school trip, perhaps? She ran through all the possibilities that sprang to mind, but no link jumped out. Normally, staff simply flush a patient's stools away and give the pediatrician a general description, but because she happened to be in the hospital, Hallett asked the nurse to save a sample so she could take a look herself. They immediately struck her as "funny similar," as if they'd come from the same person. During her conversation with Reich, Hallett noted that E. coli is sometimes found in water, but then usually only in Third World countries. Soon after, Reich's sister came over to the hospital to keep them company. As they talked, the big storm of the previous Friday came up.

"Oh my God," Reich said. "I hope nothing got in the water when the flooding hit."

Returning home that evening, Reich's sister phoned the local police detachment where she worked. A colleague mentioned she also had a child with symptoms similar to Aleasha's. In light of her chat with Cathy in the hospital, she suggested it might be the water. A small-town grapevine began humming.

With both young charges admitted and under hospital care, Hallett headed home. While she strongly suspected E. coli O157, the possibility of poisonous drinking water didn't enter her mind. Nor did she consider the possibility that she was witnessing the vanguard of a larger epidemic. With the exception of Panabaker, none of the area's family doctors or other hospitals had called to say they were having a run of sick children. Still, she was baffled by the circumstances that had brought these two youngsters under her wing. Something was definitely wrong.

Friday, May 19
8 A.M.

As she made her morning rounds, Dr. Hallett was challenged by a nurse, who had overheard the parents of the two sick children talking.

"There's more people getting sick in Walkerton," the nurse told Hallett. "And they're getting antibiotics."

"We can't treat them until we know what we're treating," Hallett replied, her voice gentle but emphatic.

Antibiotics are contraindicated in cases of E. coli poisoning, and Hallett considered calling the Walkerton hospital to advise against their use. That would be presumptuous, she thought, given she had no way of knowing what was ailing those patients. But word of the other cases roused her suspicion that some kind of outbreak was occurring. Moreover, she worried that patients were being treated wrongly out of panic.

From her involvement in its sexual health clinic, Hallett knew some of the people at the public-health unit, whose red-brick building sits almost directly behind her office. But never before had she called them to report a suspected disease outbreak. She walked over to the ward telephone and called Dr. Murray McQuigge, the region's medical officer of health. He wasn't in. Hallett decided against leaving a voicemail and was put through to his executive assistant, Mary Sellars, a helpful woman who had joined the unit as a full-time staffer a month earlier. Hallett briefly explained the situation and outlined her reasons for wanting McQuigge to consider investigating the possibility of an infectious-disease outbreak.

"Do I need to call him right away?" Sellars asked.

"No," Hallett replied, adding she just wanted the doctor to be aware that something was going on.

"I'll let him know. I'll put a note on his desk."

Roughly eight decades after Theodor von Escherich first identified E. coli, scientists unmasked the potentially lethal rogue mutant during an investigation of an outbreak caused by undercooked hamburgers: E. coli O157:H7. The O denotes the bacterium's specific type of surface; the H denotes its type of flagella, the tiny spiral-like protuberances that allow the bacterium to swim toward a food source. There are 170 O serogroups, as they're known, and many more combinations of O and H serotypes. Most are harmless. Not O157:H7, which is resistant to the stomach acid that kills its close but helpful cousins. The bacterium has an uncanny ability to latch on to the insides of the intestines, where it essentially dissolves the inner lining of the large bowel, creating a direct path to the victim's bloodstream for its deadly verotoxin. Whereas it might take 100 million other bacteria to cause disease by the intestinal route, just a dozen or so of the mutant variety can cause ghastly illness or death. It takes anywhere from one to eight days for those unlucky enough to be attacked to become ill, although symptoms typically show in three to four days. Raging diarrhea that lasts for up to ten days, sometimes longer, often turns bloody after about twenty-four hours. Excruciating abdominal pain, which suggests an inflamed or burst appendix, along with an absence of high fever typically caused by other stomach bugs, provides a telltale sign of the inner havoc being wreaked as O157 begins to spill its poison. The toxin itself does terrible damage to the cells lining the smallest blood vessels in the body, causing minuscule blockages that deprive the tissue of oxygen and nutrients. Dying tissue is what causes the agonizing pain characteristic of the illness. The damage to the blood vessels also causes blood and fluid to leak into the wall of the colon and stool, resulting in the bloody diarrhea. But what makes E. coli O157:H7 particularly frightening is that its poison, now being pumped by the heart through the bloodstream around the body, can find its way to distant organs, such as the kidneys.

There, the verotoxin destroys the lining of the millions of tiny blood vessels that act as filters to produce urine. Red blood cells forced through the damaged vessels are themselves damaged, causing almost instant anemia as internal oxygen levels begin to fall. The patient turns pale and the eyes puff from the buildup of fluid as the injured kidneys struggle to cope with the poisonous assault.

Roughly 15 per cent of those infected with E. coli develop the constellation of these symptoms that make up hemolytic uremic syndrome (HUS). Children, especially those around two years of age, and the elderly are particularly susceptible. Antibiotics don't help and may actually make things worse. All doctors can do is keep the patient hydrated. In about half of HUS cases, blood-cleansing dialysis is needed to replace the kidney function. Still, most of the time, the body eventually fights off the infection and expels the poison by itself. The damaged blood vessels repair themselves and the patient recovers fully. For an unlucky some, though, the damage is permanent. About one in ten children who recovers from the onslaught develops problems later in life as their scarred kidneys fail to grow properly. For them, regular dialysis or a transplant may become the only alternatives to death. Some don't get that far. In roughly three to five of every one hundred patients who get HUS, the verotoxin produced so far away by the bacteria in the gut makes the trip to the brain, where it causes death by a thousand tiny clots.

E. coli O157:H7 also infects cattle, particularly cows, although it causes them no grief. They do, however, become shedders, sometimes for a lifetime, spewing billions of the bugs into the environment through their feces. The tough, adaptable bacteria survive well in water or soil, perhaps for up to six months at a stretch. Anything coming into contact with the infected fecal matter becomes a potential hazard. In late 1992, a massive E. coli O157 outbreak in the northwest United States was traced to bad hamburger meat from the Jack in the Box restaurant chain. Of the 732 people who fell ill, 4 died and 195 needed hospital treatment.

North America had again been confronted by what commonly came to be thought of as the "hamburger disease." Still, large outbreaks are relatively uncommon. Canada might see about seventy-five cases of E. coli–induced HUS every year, twenty-five of those in Ontario. Most are random, sporadic events, the result of consuming bad meat, raw milk, or untreated apple cider. Swimming pools and well water have also caused small outbreaks. But never before in North America had treated drinking water from a municipal supply caused the illness.

Friday, May 19
10:30 A.M.

Kristen Hallett climbed into her car for the familiar ten-minute ride back to her office. Now and again, her eyes twitched, perhaps a sign of too little sleep so common to those in her field, perhaps a sign of deep thought. Even though her young patients were both in stable condition, she was distinctly uneasy. The message is going to sit on his desk all weekend, she thought.

At age thirty-two, Dr. Hallett had already made many life-saving decisions. She had pulled newborns from the brink of death, successfully treated kids who, by all accounts, should have died from severe internal infections. Yet the magnitude of those achievements was often submerged in the swirling emotions of parents overjoyed to learn their little ones would survive. Often, there wasn't even an opportunity for a thank you. Mostly, the parents simply didn't have a clue what she'd done. Yet Hallett, the mother of two small kids herself, took a quiet pride in her work. Nevertheless the decision she made as she swung into the parking lot behind her office that morning seemed to her, even in retrospect, to be unremarkable. She strode into her rooms and, while her patients waited, a little boy flying an oversized Fisher-Price airplane in the front corner by the windows, picked up the phone.

"I'm sorry for calling back," she told Mary Sellars. "But I think that this shouldn't sit on his desk all weekend. You have to make sure Dr. McQuigge gets the message today."

Sellars promised to act on the request. Hallett went home that Friday of the Victoria Day long weekend to prepare for a couple of days out of town. Not for a second did it occur to her that the brief phone call she had made from her office that morning would earn her national recognition as a hero.

Friday, May 19
11 A.M.

Dave Patterson was looking forward to the Victoria Day long weekend. Less than six months from retirement, the grey-haired, bespectacled Patterson had had a long career in public health, reaching the position of assistant director of health protection at the Bruce-Grey-Owen Sound public-health unit. As he settled down in expectation of a quiet day, Mary Sellars, assistant to the head of the unit, passed on a vaguely disturbing message. A Dr. Kristen Hallett had called looking for the medical officer of health. She had wanted to talk to Dr. McQuigge about two young patients, both from Walkerton, both now in the Owen Sound Hospital. What bothered Hallett, Sellars explained, was that both patients had bloody diarrhea. While calls from doctors reporting various situations or wishing to discuss concerns were not uncommon, something was unusual about this one. Bloody diarrhea is always a red flag for doctors and those in the public health field because of its link to E. coli O157. Patterson called in Bev Middleton, one of three members of his communicable diseases team.

"Bev, I want you to listen to this," Patterson said. He proceeded to play the voicemail message left by Sellars.

"Would you check with Dr. Hallett, please, and find out what's going on?"

Middleton soon reported back. Staff at the Owen Sound hospital had collected stool samples for analysis. Middleton had asked that the health unit be notified as soon as possible if the hospital lab turned up any dangerous bugs in the cultures. It would take at least twenty-four hours for the earliest preliminary

results, another day for definitive results. Given that the two youngsters were both from Walkerton, Middleton had also decided
to put out some further feelers. At the Walkerton hospital,
Dr. Michael Gill reported having seen eight similar cases over the
past two days. No one had been admitted and no one had collected any stool samples. One of the patients coming through the
emergency department was little Mary Rose Raymond, whose
diarrhea had turned bloody. She was also throwing up. She was
sent back home to Hanover with a prescription for an anti-nausea
medicine and hydration formula.

Friday, May 19
Noon

It had been one of those days for Stan Koebel. He'd spent the
morning up in Southampton at yet another meeting about a
proposed amalgamation of several area electrical utilities. His
counterpart from Hanover was driving them back when Stan's
cellphone rang. It was Janice Hallahan, who told him that James
Schmidt of the public-health unit's office in Walkerton had just
contacted her.

"It's regarding some calls that I've received about some people
being sick and I just wanted to talk to Mr. Koebel about that,"
Schmidt had said.

After being dropped off, Stan climbed into his truck and
called Schmidt, who told him that children from Mother Teresa
had come down with diarrhea and stomach cramps.

"Is there anything with the water?" Schmidt asked.

"I don't think so," Stan said. "I think the water's okay."

"Yeah, well, just checking," Schmidt said. "Probably just the
flu or some bad food or something."

Stan was bothered. What was that about? No one from the
Environment Ministry had called. Nor had he heard anything
from the lab regarding the new set of samples from the water-
main project, which had fallen still further behind schedule.
Then again, the main wasn't even hooked up to the system. He

tried to remember what was on the other fax, the one showing
the bad samples in the town's taps. But perhaps because the
notion that the water could somehow be to blame was too terrible to contemplate, he filed the idea away in the back of his mind
and headed over to the construction site on Highway 9. To his
dismay, Frank told him that they'd connected the main to Saugeen
Filter Supply and had already cracked the valve to allow water
from the town's distribution system to fill the new main. No one
would be drinking the water until the tests on the new main came
back clean, Frank explained. Stan frowned but said nothing.

In Walkerton, the humming of the grapevine was getting more
intense. From the Owen Sound hospital, Cathy Reich called her
mom, who was looking after Aleasha's big sister, who had also
come down with bloody diarrhea. Reich asked her mother to stop
giving Amanda tap water and to tell anyone else who might call
the same thing. One person who did call was another mom with
children at Mother Teresa. She immediately took bottled water
to the school for her kids. Reich's mom also called Aleasha's
great-grandmother, who lived at the Brucelea Haven nursing
home. She mentioned to a nurse that they suspected something
was in the water because Aleasha and Amanda were both ill.
Reich also phoned her husband at work, and he, too, advised his
employees against using the water.

At the health unit in Owen Sound, Middleton began con-
tacting Walkerton's schools. From staff at Mother Teresa, she
heard that numerous children had come down with diarrhea and
stomach cramps. Similar information came from a second elementary school, where absenteeism had also risen sharply. A
call to Sacred Heart high school proved an anomaly. There didn't
appear to be anything unusual among the students there.
Middleton concluded that whatever was going on, it appeared to
be affecting the younger kids, those in Grades 2, 3, and 4, rather
than the older ones. Patterson mulled over the information.
Despite the paucity of details, despite the fast-approaching long
weekend, it was becoming clearer that they had a public-health
problem on their hands that required immediate attention. As

they chatted, Middleton mentioned a strange part of her conversation with her contact at Mother Teresa.

"Is the water okay or is there something wrong with it?" she told Patterson she'd been asked.

Patterson took a deep breath.

"I'd better call the Walkerton Public Utilities Commission."

Friday, May 19
4 P.M.

Stan had just arrived back at the PUC office when Dave Patterson reached him by phone. The two men had chatted briefly once before several years earlier and barely knew each other. Patterson was feeling a little uneasy about bothering the manager with what amounted to a fishing expedition without either hook or bait.

"Has anything unusual happened recently with the town's water system?" he asked. "We've had calls from people concerned about the water and we're looking at some illness in the community."

Patterson mentioned the higher incidence of absenteeism at Mother Teresa, located on the south side of town.

"Well, there's been some water-main construction at that end of town in the past week," Stan told him. "We're flushing the mains and we put in a new chlorinator on the well yesterday."

In any event, Stan continued, the water usually tested fine even without treatment, but that wouldn't be unexpected given that it came from a deep well.

"Have you had any complaints about the water?" Patterson asked.

"Yeah, about two or three weeks ago. We had some complaints about too much chlorine," Stan said, noting he'd also heard a few hours earlier from James Schmidt.

"Anything unusual happen recently with the system?"

"Not really. The water is okay."

"It might just be the flu or food," Patterson allowed.

The topic switched to the previous Friday's big storm. A front-page newspaper photograph of a flooded street leading to a Walkerton park was still fresh in Patterson's mind.

"Could the heavy rain and flooding have had any effect on the water?" Patterson asked.

"Not likely," Stan said. "It's a closed-loop system that shouldn't be affected by a rainfall."

"Well, better keep a close eye on the chlorine levels in the construction area."

"No problem. I'll try to maintain high residuals over the weekend."

Patterson wasn't feeling much enlightened. An E. coli O157 outbreak remained a distinct possibility. But if it were E. coli, it would most likely come from food, not water. Certainly not treated water. Patterson and Middleton kicked about some ideas, possible causes. In his notebook, he jotted down E. coli, campylobacter, and salmonella. The pair also discussed viruses, but the symptoms didn't add up. As he and Middleton considered their next moves, Middleton took two more calls. Maple Court Villa, home to about 150 Walkerton retirees, reported that several residents had come down with diarrhea. They wanted additional enteric outbreak kits from the health unit so they could collect specimens. Middleton promised to provide the kits and gave the home an outbreak identification number to allow the testing laboratories to link the specimens to a particular situation. The second call was from Brucelea Haven, the town's nursing home. Several of its 135 residents had diarrhea, two with blood. Middleton asked the home to begin a line listing, a simple tracking procedure that gathers information on patients, when they began experiencing symptoms and what those were. She also provided an outbreak number and asked the home to collect specimens and keep them in a fridge until they could be picked up. With the holiday weekend about to start, a courier would be around to collect them on Tuesday morning for shipping to the lab. During the conversation, the nurse, Lisa Stroeder, mentioned that staff had heard about the ill Mother Teresa students. In addition, Dr. Michael

Gill, who acted as the home's physician besides running a general practice in town, had seen about a dozen or so patients at his office. Stroeder, whose husband worked for Aleasha Reich's dad, had concluded it couldn't be the nursing home's food.

"Is there something wrong with the water?" Stroeder asked Middleton.

Middleton relayed the question to Patterson.

"I've just got off the phone with the manager of the PUC and my understanding is that the water is fine," he said.

Middleton passed that along to Stroeder, who asked if it would be advisable for the nursing home to boil its drinking water anyway. Middleton told her that couldn't hurt. It didn't sound to Stroeder like a ringing endorsement. Still dissatisfied, she took her fears to Edythe Oberle, the home's director of nursing. Within an hour, the nursing home had removed any juices made from town water and started using boiled or bottled water, despite the added expense. Ultimately, forty-six residents of the home fell ill, but the decision to stop using tap water then and there undoubtedly spared many other of the vulnerable residents an agonizing descent into illness and death.

Patterson pondered. In and of itself, diarrhea among residents of nursing or retirement homes is not uncommon. But such outbreaks, which can be caused by several bugs, tend to be confined to the facilities. Here, however, a pattern, vague as it was, was emerging. Whatever was making people sick appeared to be hitting the very young and the very old, typical of E. coli O157. Usually, a widespread outbreak can be traced to a large gathering, a wedding or church supper perhaps, or, as had happened in 1992 with the Jack in the Box, to a restaurant. During each of her calls, Middleton had made a point of asking whether the patients had attended some kind of gathering: a school trip, a graduation dance, a party, anything that could tie them to a common event. Nothing. Moreover, the chances of the two disparate age groups sharing the same sort of food or being at a single function seemed remote. Patterson thought about the water as a possible source, but considered that highly unlikely. Never had there been an E. coli

outbreak in North America linked to a properly treated municipal water system, and Stan Koebel had told him Walkerton's water
was okay.

Had Patterson thought to familiarize himself with the town's
water file, kept in the health unit's Walkerton office, he might have
been a little less certain about Stan's assurances. The file included
numerous laboratory reports from prior to the fall of 1996, when
the Ontario government had decided to get out of the water-testing
business and leave municipalities to find private laboratories to
do the tests. Many of those reports indicated contamination of the
water. Although the regular lab reports had all but ceased after
the 1996 privatization, there was one in the file showing E. coli
in the water from as recently as August 1999. The file also contained three in-depth Environment Ministry inspection reports
from the previous decade, the last done by Michelle Zillinger in
early 1998. All documented deficiencies, including E. coli and
other contamination, failure to test the water in accordance with
provincial guidelines, and failure to disinfect it properly. The file
was kept in the Walkerton office run by James Schmidt, the unit's
on-the-ground inspector and a self-described dedicated employee
with a conscience and a passion for public health. His practice
was to glance at the incoming documents, if he had the time,
put them in a file, and forget about them. If there were problems
with Walkerton's water, he figured, that was the Environment
Ministry's concern.

Friday, May 19
4:20 P.M.

From head office in Owen Sound came the request to James
Schmidt to deliver outbreak kits to Maple Court Villa. They had
a need for them, was all he was told. He didn't ask any questions. About the same time, a woman called to tell him about
the illnesses at Mother Teresa. He told her he'd already heard
from the school and that he was looking into it. Schmidt gathered up the outbreak kits and delivered them to Maple Court

Villa, then turned his mind to the long weekend and headed home to nearby Hanover, where Patterson reached him just as he walked in the door. Patterson relayed what he had been hearing throughout the day.

"Has anything happened in or around Walkerton that would have involved a large group of people?" Patterson asked.

"Not that I know about," Schmidt replied.

The history of E. coli contamination in Walkerton's water system contained in the file stashed away somewhere in Schmidt's office never came up. He never thought to mention its contents, not that he remembered them anyway, and no one at the health unit head office thought to ask.

At the PUC, long-time clerical worker Viv Slater went over to Stan.

"I've had calls asking if the water's okay," she said. "Small kids have been getting sick. And Maple Court called as well."

"I can't understand how it could be the water," Stan said.

He went to have a chat with Hallahan. They're probably dealing with a flu epidemic, he said, not sounding particularly worried. Still, he told Hallahan, he'd go out and check the chlorinator at Well 7 to make sure it was working properly. Perhaps, somehow, the water-main project had contaminated the system, although that was highly unlikely. But the uneasy feeling gnawing at him was taking on a new urgency. Sick children? The last thing in the world Stan Koebel needed was a problem with the water, especially one that would become public. Not with all the other stuff going on and the uncertainty over what would happen to the waterworks with the hydro side leaving. It wouldn't look good.

Never before had Stan flushed the town's water system after a single bad test result. Still, he figured, if there was a problem, flushing and increasing chlorine levels would surely fix it. He might have given more thought to the fact that Well 7 had pumped unchlorinated water into the system for almost the entire week, but he didn't. He got into the truck and headed over to the PUC shop. It was late afternoon and he wondered if he'd find anyone still there. He pulled onto the gravel in front of the rectangular single-storey shop, its grey aluminum siding glinting

dully in the afternoon sun. To his relief, he spotted Frank, who
was just getting ready to call it quits for the week. As he and Al
Buckle walked toward their cars, Frank noticed that Stan looked
even more worried than he had earlier in the afternoon.

"We've got a problem out here on Highway 9," Stan told him,
absent-mindedly pointing in the direction of the construction
site. "They're still getting bad samples. We gotta do a bunch of
flushing this weekend. I'm going to start on a couple of hydrants
right now."

Frank couldn't see what the big deal was.

"How'd it go with the chlorinator?" Stan asked.

"It's up and running," Frank replied. "Got it done this
morning."

"Good."

Al Buckle hesitated for a couple of minutes, figuring there
might be some overtime in the offing, but Stan didn't ask.

"See youse later," said Buckle, who got into his car and drove
off, leaving the two brothers alone.

"I'm pretty worried about all these bad samples that are
coming back," Stan went on as Buckle's car disappeared from
sight. "They say it's in the distribution."

Frank was quiet.

"People calling the office this afternoon asking about the
water," Stan continued. "Some kids getting sick. Even got a call
from the public health guys. They wanted to know if the water
was safe. Said it was okay."

Stan wanted desperately to make Frank understand that this
was different. Serious, even. There was something in the water.
Bacteria. More than ever, he wanted his younger brother, to
whom he had so often turned with water questions, to understand
just how worried he was, to say or do something to make it right.
Frank considered.

"No way that can be," Frank said. "It can't be the water."

"They're saying it is."

"Can't be."

"Well, I'm going to start flushing and upping the chlorine
tonight anyway."

Above: Dr. Kristen Hallett, a pediatrician in Owen Sound, sparked an intense hunt for a stealth attacker after being puzzled by an unusual coincidence of symptoms in two young patients.

Top right: Dave Patterson, of the public health unit, received almost no recognition for his role in discovering what was befalling Walkerton and advising residents to boil their water.

Bottom right: Dr. Murray McQuigge shares a moment with his wife Cory during the judicial inquiry. The outspoken medical officer of health took most of the glory for solving the E. coli mystery.

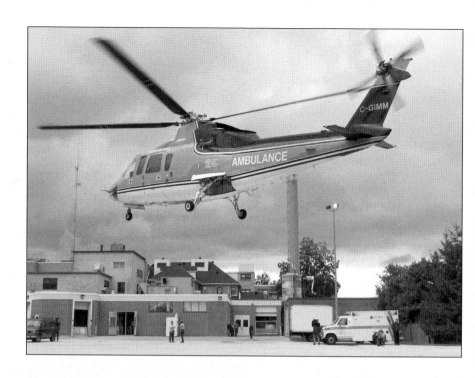

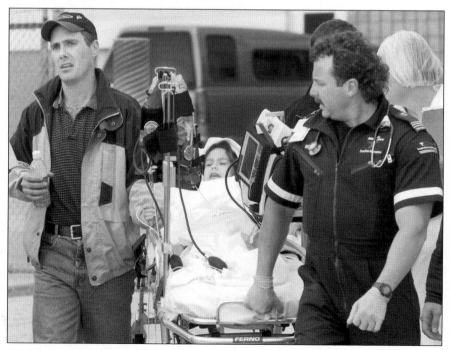

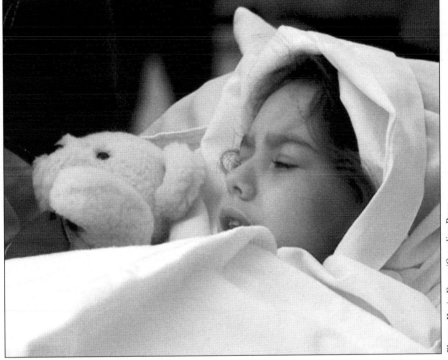

Photos: Kevin Frayer/Canadian Press

Accompanied by her teddy bear, Tamara Smith watches apprehensively as she is wheeled to a waiting helicopter. This photograph was seen around the world.

Opposite page top: An evacuation helicopter takes off from the Walkerton hospital. The sound of the choppers, used to ferry only the most seriously ill, still haunts those who heard them.

Opposite page bottom: A distraught Brad Smith helps paramedics rush his five-year-old daughter Tamara to a helicopter for an emergency airlift to London from Walkerton hospital.

Pallbearers carry the casket of Edith Pearson from Sacred Heart Catholic Church. The deaths of seven people and illnesses of 2,300 others from E. coli poisoning rocked the town.

Ontario Premier Mike Harris listens to questions from reporters outside Walkerton's municipal offices as anxious residents watch. In the background, Dieter Weiss holds his sign.

Photos: Kevin Frayer/Canadian Press

Holocaust survivor and nascent activist Phil Englishman joins other angry town residents in demanding information about the crisis and its cause from the mayor.

Top left: Businessman Jim Kieffer was acclaimed to the Walkerton Public Utilities Commission four times. As PUC chairman, he trusted Stan Koebel to look after the town's water.

Top right: Veterinarian Dave Biesenthal and Night of the Storm. In 1978, the Walkerton PUC located a shallow well next to his farm. The consequences two decades later were disastrous.

Bottom left: Bruce Davidson co-founded the group Concerned Walkerton Citizens. Dubbed a quote machine, here he talks to reporters covering a big protest that never happened.

Bottom right: Walkerton's mayor, Dave Thomson, faced pointed criticism about his handling of the unfolding water crisis, which he appeared to ignore for almost two full days.

Jim Rankin/*Toronto Star*

Above: Stan Koebel, with daughter
Stephanie McQueen. Here, the water
manager listens as lawyer Bill Trudell
pleads for the public to suspend judgment on the cause of the E. coli tragedy.

Brent Davis/*The Record*, Kitchener, Ontario

Right: Frank Koebel, foreman
of the Walkerton Public Utilities
Commission, leaves after telling
a judicial inquiry he didn't
believe in chlorination and he
falsified safety records.

Ontario Appeal Court Justice Dennis O'Connor headed the comprehensive judicial inquiry into the disaster. His fairness, sensitivity and gentle humour endeared him to the people of Walkerton.

"Hell, it can wait till Tuesday."

Frank could see Stan wanted him to help. But he had other plans for the evening. He didn't offer and Stan didn't ask.

"I'll give you hand tomorrow," Frank said, and off he went.

Friday, May 19
5:30 P.M.

Stan grabbed some equipment and drove the few blocks to Mother Teresa. He opened the hydrant out front. With its location at the south end of town, flushing there would allow the system to draw fresh chlorinated water from Well 7. Stan's digital chlorine analyser registered a barely detectible level of the chemical. As water gushed from the hydrant, he headed west along Highway 9, past the water tower, past the Biesenthal farm, turned right at the next concession, and pulled up at Well 7. He was there when Hallahan, who had stopped at her parents' house after running some pre-weekend errands, reached him on his cellphone.

"Just wanted to make sure everything's okay," she said. "Do you need me to do anything?"

"No, no. Everything looks fine, but I'm flushing and increasing the chlorination levels, just to be sure."

Bob McKay was taking it easy resting his bum knee when his wife, Brenda, came home with the children. Their piano teacher had mentioned that a couple of dozen kids were ill at Mother Teresa and had asked her if she'd heard anything similar, which Brenda hadn't. Bob didn't give it much thought. A little while later, he headed out to the PUC shop looking to borrow a tool to inflate the tire on his riding lawnmower. There was no one around. But he did notice that a fire hydrant across the street from the shop had a length of hose on it. The hydrant was open.

"Kind of odd they're flushing out a water main after hours on a long weekend," he told Brenda when he got home.

Then it struck him: Could the flushing be connected to the failed Highway 9 samples Frank had told him about the previous day and the sick kids Brenda had mentioned? He made a decision: The family stopped drinking the water.

At Well 7, Stan found the chlorine levels looking pretty good. At least the new chlorinator was working properly. He cranked it up anyway and headed back to the open hydrant at the school. By 7 P.M., the chlorine level there had risen a notch. It had been a long day and Stan decided to head home for a quick bite and some brief down time. It didn't last. JoAnn Todd, director of the Maple Court Villa seniors residence, was on the phone.

"I've heard rumours the water's unfit," Todd said.

"The water's okay," Stan replied. "It comes from a deep well so it can't be contaminated."

Stan Koebel cut a lonely figure that Friday evening as he made several more trips to the hydrant outside Mother Teresa. Each time, the chlorine levels were higher. He didn't really have a clear idea of what reading he wanted, but the digital analyser was starting to show a good amount in the system. He shut the hydrant down and headed back one more time to the pumphouse in the darkness, where a quick test showed high levels of the disinfectant. It was 11 o'clock on the Friday night of the Victoria Day long weekend when the troubled manager of Walkerton's Public Utilities Commission headed home.

9

In Search of a Hidden Attacker

Saturday, May 20
11 A.M..

INSTEAD OF RELAXING on the long weekend, Dave Patterson was searching for answers. The Owen Sound hospital laboratory had just reported that stool cultures from one of the two children referred to Dr. Kristen Hallett were showing signs of E. coli O157, although the analysis had yet to be confirmed. The second case appeared normal. Patterson immediately called Bev Middleton at home to ask her to check the Walkerton hospital for an update. A few minutes later, Middleton was able to tell him that the emergency department there was full. Ten children and as many adults had been seen. Two were ill enough to be admitted. Another thirty or so people had called asking for information. Six stool specimens had been collected, but the one result they had so far was negative. The hospital also told Middleton that some of the patients had been asking about the town's water.

"I think you'd better head to the office and fax down the three fact sheets that we have on HUS and E. coli to the hospital," Patterson told Middleton. "Oh, better check with Hanover as well. Just tell them what's going on, and send them the faxes too."

Patterson hung up and called James Schmidt at home to bring him up to date. Given the comments from the patients in the Walkerton hospital about the water, he asked Schmidt to call Stan Koebel again.

"Ask him about the levels of chlorine in the system. Also, check whether they're keeping a close eye on the water there. And let him know we have more illnesses."

Saturday morning's dawn had found Stan Koebel back at Well 7. He could smell the chlorine. As the orange sun peeped over the horizon, he headed over to Mother Teresa yet again and opened the hydrant. A little later, Frank joined him for a spell, and the two brothers opened several other hydrants at various locations. Around town, the water gushed. Around town, people were doubling over in pain and rushing to the washroom. At midmorning, with levels in the water towers plunging, Well 5 kicked in automatically and began pumping. Stan went over to the well. The chlorine levels looked good. And then it was back to check the hydrants. It was hot work. Now and again, he filled his hard hat with water from a hydrant to quench his thirst. The ring of his cellphone interrupted his reverie.

"Hi, Stan. How ya doin'?" Schmidt asked. "What's going on?"

"Well, we're flushing the lines," Stan replied, the sounds of gushing water audible in the background. "We've just replaced the chlorinator and done some mains work."

"Anything else? Any other unusual events you can let me know about or tell me? Is everything okay with the system?"

"No, no. Everything's okay," Stan replied.

Schmidt asked about the chlorine levels and noted down Stan's responses. It didn't occur to him to ask about the chlorinator or why Stan had replaced it. Nor did it strike him as odd that Stan was out flushing a water main on the Saturday morning of a long weekend. Nor did it occur to him that there might be a connection between the reports of illness and what Stan was doing. The call, however, left Stan rattled. He drove over to the PUC office and went to his desk. From under a pile of papers, he fished out the lab results from the previous week. He sat down and, for the first time, studied them closely. It looked really bad. But hell, if it was that bad, surely the lab would have passed the results on to the Ministry of the Environment? And surely the ministry would have given him a call? In any event, there was no need to panic. The flushing and extra chlorine would take care of any problems. Stan took some time out to help his daughter fill their backyard swimming pool and get it ready for the season. He took a swig from the garden hose every now and again.

Saturday, May 20
Noon

Bob McKay was fretting. The unusual flushing he had witnessed and his wife's mention of the sick kids had nagged at him through the previous evening and into the morning. Over the backyard fence, his neighbour mentioned hearing from Cathy Reich that two or three kids had been taken to Owen Sound hospital with blood in their stool. Reich had also passed on her suspicions about the cause.

"Could there be something wrong with the water?" asked the neighbour, whose own daughter had also taken ill.

"It's a possibility," McKay told her. "Anything's possible." Her family, too, stopped drinking from the taps.

Just before lunch, McKay noticed another hydrant being flushed near Mother Teresa. Again, there was no one in sight. What was going on? Someone should come and check things out, he thought. He headed home and called his mother.

"Mom, what should I do?" he asked, after explaining what was bothering him and what he had in mind.

"Bob," she said, "you do the right thing."

Had his relationship with his boss been better, McKay might simply have picked up the phone and called Stan Koebel. But it had always been clear to him that Stan, or Frank for that matter, didn't much like being questioned. Steve Lorley had once said to him, "You do as you're told, you'll be fine here." Besides, the layoff threats and ensuing unpleasantness made such a call impossible, especially when his suspicions might prove groundless. No. Calling Stan wasn't an option. McKay scanned the Blue Pages of the phone directory until he found the number for the Ministry of the Environment office in Owen Sound. A recording referred him to the ministry's emergency hotline, the Spills Action Centre, in Toronto. At 12:20 P.M. on Saturday, May 20, McKay called the hotline, where he reached Chris Johnson, a recent graduate who had been hired full-time just weeks earlier. As the new kid on the ministry block, the long weekend shift fell to young Chris.

"Spills Action Centre speaking."

McKay gulped.

"Yes, um, I'm just wondering if I could, ah, file, a complaint on a new system going in, you know what I mean?"

"Okay," said Johnson. "What's your name?"

What if there was nothing to his suspicions?

"I don't wish to give that," McKay said, not for a moment thinking that call-display technology at the centre could render his attempt at anonymity moot.

Instead, McKay talked about the failed samples Frank had mentioned two days earlier and the hydrant flushing he'd seen. In his nervousness, he forgot to bring up what he'd heard of kids being ill. After getting numbers for Stan and Frank Koebel from McKay, Johnson promised to look into it. It was early Saturday afternoon that Stan received a message from the PUC answering service to return a call to the Spills Action Centre in Toronto. He had no idea what the centre was but called anyway, using its toll-free phone number.

"Uh, I had a complaint of adverse water samples taken in the Walkerton area on the new main they are putting in," Johnson told Stan.

"Okay, which new main?"

Johnson said he didn't know. Instead, he asked a few basic questions, such as whether Walkerton had its own water-treatment plant and how to contact its operator.

"You're talking to him," Stan replied. "These samples: who brought them down?" he asked, still unclear to whom he was talking or where they were located.

"Um, well, what I got was an anonymous call. I'm in Toronto."

Stan told him they had two or three different mains under construction. He said he'd been flushing since 5 P.M. the previous day and that the chlorine residuals seemed fine.

"Okay, this complaint was for the water samples on Thursday. Said a lot of them failed. It was an anonymous complaint," Johnson went on. "So I take it as an anonymous complaint."

"Okay," Stan replied. "So we're not sure if it was that or not?"

"No. I just wanted to inquire and find out what's going on."

"Yeah. We have a fair bit of construction and there's some concern. Um. I'm not sure. We're not finding anything, but I'm doing this as a precaution."

"So, you haven't had any adverse samples then?" Johnson asked suddenly.

"Um, we've had the odd one, you know," Stan said, his voice rising slightly. "We're in the process of changing companies because the other company had closed the doors. So we're going through some pains right now to get it going."

Stan didn't mention the disturbing laboratory reports, which had been lying on his desk unheeded for almost three full days, even though he'd studied them just a scant few hours earlier. He said nothing about the test results showing serious contamination of the town's drinking water, contamination that included potentially lethal E. coli. The secret, the fear, the worry stayed bottled up. He had tried to share it with Frank a day earlier, to no avail. There was no one to help now. So Stan Koebel kept quiet. And he kept flushing. No one need ever know.

Saturday, May 20
I P.M.

The sense of unease Dave Patterson felt was getting stronger. Still nothing definitive. Still no clear cause. Then he heard from a Walkerton mother, worried because her daughter had used the drinking fountain a day earlier at Mother Teresa and a teacher had warned the child not to do that. Patterson told her the health unit was aware of a diarrhea outbreak and was in touch with the hospital. They had also talked to the public utilities commission and had been told the water was fine. He'd barely put the phone down when the Walkerton hospital called to say that someone had come in and said a local radio station was warning people against drinking the water. There had in fact been no such broadcast, but the town's grapevine had gone into overdrive and, as is to be expected, the message had become garbled. Patterson, of course, knew nothing about such a report. And again he simply relayed what Stan Koebel had told him: the water, apparently, was fine, but he promised to investigate further. A quick check with the laboratory turned up nothing new. Remembering that he had yet to hear from James Schmidt, Patterson called him at his Hanover home and left a message asking him to take the ten-minute drive over to Walkerton to check the chlorine levels in the town's tap water himself. Patterson was deeply worried. It was time to involve Dr. Murray McQuigge, the head of the health unit. His boss wasn't going to be pleased to be disturbed at the cottage, but it had to be done.

A day earlier, McQuigge and his wife, Cory, who had just been diagnosed with breast cancer, prepared for the approaching long weekend by loading their car and heading for the refuge of the family cottage in Muskoka. It would be the ideal place to spend some much needed time together, to relax, to enjoy a benignly busy unofficial start to the summer. A quick check with the office had turned up nothing out of the ordinary and the medical officer of health had begun to put the worries of the workaday world behind him. It was to be a short-lived respite. McQuigge was puttering around his cottage when the phone rang. Dave Patterson apologized for disturbing him and laid out the grim, unfolding puzzle he was facing. One presumed case of E. coli, the child in Owen Sound, and as many as thirty cases of bloody diarrhea in the Walkerton area, one also showing preliminary signs of E. coli poisoning. Most of the illnesses were from Walkerton, but nothing seemed to tie them together. McQuigge expressed his satisfaction with the steps the health unit had taken. Nevertheless, he said, if any other cases of E. coli turned up, they should start interviewing the patients directly for more information.

"Look, there's something very wrong here," Patterson pleaded. "You should come back."

There was a long pause.

"Okay," McQuigge sighed. "I'll head back."

McQuigge broke the news to his wife and the couple packed up and began the long drive home. Their planned weekend getaway had lasted less than twenty-four hours. In the interim, Schmidt had arrived at the health unit office in Walkerton, where he had attempted, without success, to detect chlorine in the tap water. He called Patterson to tell him, adding that he'd go out and check the levels at other locations. He also mentioned that his wife, a nurse at the Hanover hospital, had told him of patients from both the town and nearby Durham who all had similar symptoms to those in Walkerton and Owen Sound. Patterson decided to call Stan Koebel a second time. Once again, the water manager explained he was flushing mains. Once again he mentioned finding reasonable levels of chorine in the drinking water. Once again, he made no mention of the lab report he'd just finished studying. Overall, it sounded to Patterson as if everything was working normally. He suddenly remembered the comment from the Walkerton hospital about the person who had mentioned hearing something about the water on the radio.

"Maybe you should call the radio station and let everyone know things are okay, Stan," Patterson said.

Perhaps it was his own anxiety, perhaps it was his own unwillingness to believe that the manager of a town's water treatment plant might be withholding critical information, but Patterson's spur-of-the-moment suggestion really didn't make much sense.

It was quiet on the other end of the line. There was no way on earth Stan was going to make a call like that.

"I'm not very good at public speaking, but I'll see what I can do," Stan answered after a long pause.

Patterson hung up and checked his voicemail, where he found a message from Schmidt, who said he'd had no luck detecting any chlorine in any of the town's water. However, because part of his work related to public swimming pools, all Schmidt had was a standard kit familiar to any homeowner with a pool in the backyard. These kits are not sensitive to the low levels of chlorine ordinarily used to disinfect drinking water. Municipal systems barely entered the health unit's realm of activity or consciousness. Just to be sure his kit was working properly, Schmidt had actually shown some rare initiative by taking it along to the public swimming pool in Hanover, where he tested the water and got a reading. He then asked the pool attendant to check their records to see if they jibed with what he'd found. They did. The fact that Schmidt could detect no chlorine bothered Patterson, but he nevertheless felt somewhat reassured by what he'd heard from Stan Koebel, who was undoubtedly using more sensitive equipment. Chlorine, Patterson knew, is a potent bacterial disinfectant and conventional wisdom was such that as long as there's a detectable level to be found, the water must be safe to drink. Nothing in his experience suggested otherwise.

Saturday, May 20
6 P.M.

Dr. Murray McQuigge arrived back home in Kemble northwest of Owen Sound and immediately called Patterson. The Walkerton hospital had logged over a hundred calls from people inquiring about diarrhea in family members. About half mentioned bloody diarrhea. Thirty people had shown up at the hospital seeking attention, although no one had been admitted. That was one positive, McQuigge thought. He and Patterson discussed the possibility of a food-borne outbreak that could be tracked to Walkerton itself, given that people outside the town had also been affected. A suspicion the outbreak was water-related kept surfacing, but Patterson reminded his superior that Koebel had said the water was okay.

"We are worried about the water supply, despite reassurances," McQuigge jotted down in his notepad.

Patterson continued to brood over the mystery. Was it even a Walkerton outbreak? What could be causing it? Then it suddenly occurred to him:

"Dig out water system file," he wrote down, but he promptly forgot to ask for it.

Later that evening, Patterson called his immediate supervisor to let him know that he'd spoken to McQuigge and that they were awaiting additional lab results. Factoring in the incubation time for E. coli O157, the two men began trying to pinpoint the start of the outbreak, and came up with an event on the Mother's Day weekend, perhaps May 14 or 15.

Saturday, May 20
9 P.M.

Bob McKay had spent the afternoon lounging around the house, taking time out to check that the flushing at Mother Teresa was continuing. As the day wore on, his conversation with Chris Johnson at the Spills Action Centre nagged at him. They didn't seem to have had any idea that there had been bad samples. Surely the ministry should have known about them? McKay had himself developed a mild case of diarrhea. His daughter had also been having tummy problems for a couple of days. He was becoming increasingly antsy, wondering whether his whole family was falling ill. He had checked at the school again earlier in the evening. The hydrant was still open. He could stand the anxiety no more. It was 9:30 P.M. Saturday when he decided to call the ministry hotline again.

"I hope you know what you're doing," Brenda said.

At the Spills Action Centre, Brian Park answered the call. McKay said he'd phoned that afternoon and this time, he mentioned his own illness and relayed the information he'd heard from Brenda about the twenty-five sick students.

"I just wondered if something was being done about this," McKay said.

"Um," came the response.

"I'll take a water sample tonight, if you want me to do that," McKay offered.

Park ignored the suggestion, asking instead about the sick children. McKay explained the illnesses had begun a day earlier, that kids had gone to hospital with blood in the stool. Park pulled up the earlier report filed by Chris Johnson and told McKay that the action centre had spoken to someone in charge of the Walkerton works department.

"John Strader?" McKay asked, suddenly afraid the ministry had wasted its time talking to the man in charge of the town's roads and sewers rather than its tap water.

"No it was a John *Koebel*," Park said.

"*Stan* Koebel."

"Ah, no, it says *John*, who is the manager of the Walkerton Public Utilities Commission," Park insisted.

There wasn't much use arguing the point. How to make these people understand the gravity of the situation? McKay repeated his concern about the illnesses.

"That's not normal," he said for emphasis.

Park advised him to call the Health Ministry, although McKay was pretty sure the people he really wanted were from the Environment Ministry. Still, he wrote down the number Park provided.

"Is there any avenue I can take here, other than talking to you?" McKay asked one more time, his frustration and despair rising in lockstep.

"Well, you could contact the city of Walkerton. Have you done that yet?"

"Ha, forget that!"

"You don't want to do that, eh?"

"No, no. You might as well be hitting yourself against a . . . you know."

"They won't listen to you?"

"No, no."

"I see. Yeah. Your best bet is Ministry of Health because they're the ones that regulate drinking water quality."

Park, an employee of the Environment Ministry, was wrong of course and McKay knew it. When it came to drinking water, they were God. Still, he called the number Park had given him, only to be greeted by a strange recording. In his haste to dial, he'd forgotten to use the area code. So after calling back the hotline in Toronto to check the number, he reached the public-health unit for Simcoe County in Barrie. There, the call-taker told him that Walkerton was out of their area. Call the health unit in Owen Sound, McKay was told. Tired of getting the runaround and increasingly worried about what was going on in town, McKay called the Spills Action Centre one last time. It was now almost 10 P.M. Saturday.

"It's Bob from Walkerton," he said, letting his guard slip. "I got absolutely nowhere with that number. Now if you could please just do something, get rolling on this. That's all I ask, okay?"

Park promised to have the local Environment Ministry office in Owen Sound follow up. Hoping to spur quicker action, McKay mentioned that the Walkerton waterworks was using an unlicensed operator, although he didn't mention Al Buckle's name. A local inspector would look into it, Park said.

"Can you leave my first name off that?" McKay asked hopefully.

Saturday, May 20
10:30 P.M.

At the Legion hall near the Tim Hortons, Stephanie Smith was enjoying the wedding reception for a friend on her volleyball team. Everyone seemed to know the water was bad. A short distance away, Stan Koebel was giving up on another day of flushing and worrying. Nearby, Fred Pearson was fretting over his eighty-three-year-old wife, Edith. She'd been to emergency after a day of terrible cramps and bloody diarrhea, but they'd sent her home with instructions to drink plenty of fluids. In Owen Sound, Mary Rose Raymond had been admitted to hospital with tummy troubles. In a nearby bed, Aleasha Reich seemed slightly better.

10

Burning Questions, Boiling Water

Sunday, May 21
9:50 A.M.

THE MEDICINE Jamie and Cathy McDonald had given their children appeared to have worked. So, with Ian and Kylie feeling somewhat better, the family headed to Hanover for church services, where something odd happened: a teenager asked Pastor Merv Brockwell to offer a prayer for the water of Walkerton. Strange as the request seemed, Brockwell did as asked. The McDonalds looked at each other and frowned. They decided to stop drinking their tap water. At the Becker's round the corner from his house in Walkerton, travelling salesman Todd Huntley picked up his Sunday newspaper. A girl at the slush machine was filling a plastic cup with the icy, sugary, bright purple mixture. The woman behind the counter went over to her.

"Sorry, my dear," she said. "You can't buy that. The water's no good."

The girl frowned.

"Where'd you hear that from?" Huntley asked the clerk.

"Oh, a policeman just came in and said the water's bad."

Huntley didn't know what to make of it. Word of the mounting incidence of illness in the town had yet to reach him. He was just about to leave when another officer walked in. He, too, knew about the bad water.

"Who told you?" Huntley asked.

"I just hear it," the cop said.

Newspaper in hand, Huntley went home. He soon forgot the odd conversations in the convenience store. But forgetting wasn't an option for Dave Patterson. It seemed like his head had barely hit the pillow when he had to drag himself out of bed again. From his kitchen, he touched base with James Schmidt and was contemplating his next move when Murray McQuigge called. CKNX radio in Wingham was looking for information on Walkerton's water. McQuigge had told them the health unit was investigating a spate of illnesses in the town. He asked Patterson to canvas area hospitals to see if they could ascertain the hometowns of the patients displaying the by now familiar symptoms. A check with Bev Middleton revealed that she had spoken again to a nurse at the Walkerton hospital who had come on duty at 7 A.M. Five people with bloody diarrhea had come through that morning and ten others had called about similar symptoms. No one new had been admitted. The excruciatingly uncomfortable waits in the emergency room were growing longer.

"People are angry," the nurse told Middleton.

Hanover hospital had also seen another dozen patients over the past day, the Owen Sound hospital two new ones. All the patients in the three hospitals were from Walkerton. The exception was little Mary Rose Raymond, who lived in Hanover, although Middleton learned from her mom that the family had eaten in a restaurant in Walkerton on Mother's Day a week earlier. At last, Patterson thought, whatever was causing the outbreak must originate in the town.

Minutes later, another piece of the puzzle slipped into place. The Owen Sound laboratory confirmed its earlier presumptive result on one of Kristen Hallett's patients: it was E. coli O157 making the youngster ill. In addition, tests on a second patient were showing early signs of E. coli poisoning. There was little doubt now. The search that had started two days earlier pointed squarely in one direction: an E. coli outbreak that had started in Walkerton.

Sunday, May 21
Noon

Dave Patterson reviewed his notes. Nothing obvious appeared to tie together the high incidence of E. coli–induced illness among the young and old or the widespread nature of the outbreak. There had been no single event that could account for a food source. On the list of suspect sources, that put water on top, the tap water supplied by the municipality through its public utilities commission headed by Stan Koebel. Patterson mulled over Stan's contention that the water was okay, but his discomfort had grown to a near certainty that something was terribly wrong. The time for waiting for definitive answers was over.

Advising people to boil their drinking water is not without its risks. For one thing, there's a very real danger of accidents leading to burns or scald injuries. An advisory can cause anxiety and have a devastating effect on businesses, such as restaurants, and on tourism. If, ultimately, it turned out to have been unnecessary, people would be furious at the disruption to their daily lives and the health unit's credibility would take a serious hit. Still, there seemed no way around it. With Murray McQuigge's agreement, Dave Patterson sat down at his kitchen table, picked up a pen, and began writing what would undoubtedly be among the most important paragraphs of his life:

"Although the Walkerton PUC is not aware of any problems with their water system, this advisory is being issued by the health unit as a precaution until more information is known about the illness and the status of the water supply."

As Patterson worked on the wording, McQuigge called the man who had hired him as medical officer of health a decade earlier. Mayor Dave Thomson had been reeve of Brant Township and a member of the county's board of health when the then middle-aged doctor applied for the area's top public-health job. Armed with a fresh degree in public health from Harvard after twenty years as a family doctor in Lunenburg, Nova Scotia, McQuigge impressed the board as a knowledgeable professional and they hired him immediately. Despite being a small-town Ontario boy himself, McQuigge couldn't have been more different from Thomson in approach. Brash, brimming with confidence, and possessed of a highly developed sense of self, the bull-necked McQuigge struck the slightly built, soft-spoken Thomson as a man very much in control of himself. And yet both men shared something a little less obvious beneath their vastly different exteriors: a steely ego. Over the years, they ran into each other fairly often at various meetings but, beyond that, had few dealings. Until, that is, there was a salmonella outbreak in the mid-1990s in a county hospital. McQuigge came out swinging against the poultry industry. The investigation ultimately led to the destruction of thousands of hens at a barn in the United States, even though the actual contamination was found to be in improperly cleaned mixers in the hospital kitchen. The farmer in Thomson bristled. He felt McQuigge had gone too far too quickly in tarring and feathering the entire poultry industry, a key agricultural player in Bruce County. As far as Thomson was concerned, the outbreak had nothing to do with the poor hens.

"I really didn't appreciate you going around and blaming somebody till you knew who it was," Thomson told the doctor.

When McQuigge later made a big production about ordering a cleanup after a fire at a mobile-trailer park, Thomson's image of him as an intemperate man with a barely controlled temper solidified.

Dave Thomson, it is fair to say, was not a worldly man. His life revolved around the mixed cattle, hog, and sheep farm in Brant Township on which he was born and raised, the only boy among four sisters. He had attended a one-room school. Only when it came time for Grade 8 in the fall of 1945 did the country boy head to the big city, Walkerton, where he was to stay with his father's sisters. But even on the first day of high school, the routine of the farm tugged at him. There was hay to bring in, the second cut of alpha-alpha, and at noon he phoned his mom and said he'd be happy to come home and help if they'd come and get him. They did. The next morning, he said, "I think I'll just stay at home and help you." He never did get back to school. One day, a neighbour, who was on council in Brant Township, asked the fifteen-year-old Thomson to be his part-time superintendent, looking after the two roads in his section, one of which ran to the boy's family farm. He jumped at the chance. For a couple of years, young Davey helped put up snow fences, break the roads in winter, or use a pony grader to grade them in the summer. Then he spent a year as the second man on a two-man snowplough, raising or lowering the wing before moving up to the driver's seat. When his folks moved into town, he took over the farm. A year later, he married Helen, and they raised four sons, three of whom still farm in the area.

Great uncle Sandy had been something of an entrepreneur in his day and had achieved some measure of fame and fortune by designing a steel horse collar. Unlike padded collars, these were impervious to sparks and he had great success selling the contraptions to fire departments in the northern U.S. Now some folk said they weren't much good because they made the horses sweat, but when the Great War erupted, sales of the fire- and bullet-proof collars shot up. The Thomsons began buying property. Later, they would provide the financing for others in the area to buy their own farms. The Thomsons prospered. In 1966, with the oldest boy in the earliest grades, it was getting to be time to do away with the one-room school of Thomson's youth. Some people wanted to build a new consolidated school smack in the middle of the township, but trucking kids to the middle of nowhere in the winter seemed like a fool idea to Thomson. Better, he thought, would be to build in Walkerton, near the high school. That way, one school bus, whose canary yellow colour was slowly becoming familiar, could take all the kids at once. Thomson ran for school trustee, and was elected in the fall of 1966. Within two years, Brant Central opened across from the public high school

in Walkerton. When a neighbour wanted to run for the new consolidated school board, Thomson, his mission complete, decided
to step aside and put his name in for council. He was elected as
a Brant Township councillor in the fall of 1968, beginning a
career in local politics that would span five decades.

Sunday, May 21
12:40 P.M.

"**W**e've got stool cultures showing E. coli O157. It's a deadly
serious bug," McQuigge was saying. "Can you think of any food-
borne sources?"

There was pause as Thomson consulted in the background with
his son, who told him about the volunteer firefighters' Backstreet
Boys "tribute" concert at the Walkerton arena a week earlier.

"A lot of families were at that," Thomson offered.

"I hadn't heard that," McQuigge said. "Do you know what
food was served?"

Thomson consulted his son again before telling McQuigge
that pop and pizza had been available.

"Those aren't likely sources of O157," McQuigge said.

He also said the public utilities commission, whose board
Thomson sat on as mayor, had reassured the health unit that the
water was safe.

"Look, I don't want to send off any alarm bells, David,"
McQuigge went on, "but I'm going to issue a boil-water advisory
just as a precaution because we don't have a clue what this is.
There's different people sick."

After thirty-four years in local politics, Mayor Dave Thomson
was used to being called at his farm home. You learn pretty
quickly in small-town or rural public life: if people have questions
or want to complain about something, they grab you on the
street or pick up the phone and get you at home. Thomson didn't
mind particularly, although he hated being disturbed on Sundays.
Still, McQuigge's call was highly unusual. Thomson wasn't sure

what to make of it. He detected no urgency in McQuigge's voice. The doctor sounded his typical self: forceful, imposing. If he didn't want to send off any alarm bells and the boil-water advisory was just a precaution, why bother? But that was McQuigge for you. Always going off half-cocked, just like he'd done with the hens. Whatever was going on, the health unit would take care of it. If there was bad food some place, it was up to McQuigge and his crew to find it. Still, Thomson called Stan Koebel at home.

"Is the water okay, Stan?" Thomson asked. "I hear there's people getting sick."

"I think the water's okay," Stan replied.

There was no point mentioning the bad test results. By Tuesday, anyway, everything would undoubtedly be fine. Thomson shook his head and went back to enjoying his Sunday with his family. For two days, he would make no effort to find out what was happening in his town, no effort to help warn its many unsuspecting residents.

Sunday, May 21
12:52 P.M.

As head of the public-health unit, it fell to Dr. Murray McQuigge to issue the warning to people to boil their drinking water. Patterson had read his kitchen-table draft to him over the phone and McQuigge had transcribed it. But how to ensure the public would hear it, given the long weekend? The obvious answer appeared to be a local radio station. In this part of the world, radio is a key means by which people get information. Its immediacy and wide listenership make it an ideal medium for letting people know what the weather will bring or about school-bus cancellations, a relatively frequent occurrence in the county. The health unit had previously used radio to disseminate information about rabies and meningitis outbreaks as well as for previous boil-water advisories issued for two smaller towns in the region, Wiarton and Meaford. The emergency plan for the Bruce nuclear power plant on the western edge of the county depends heavily on radio. McQuigge had recently been involved in the plant's Y2K millennium bug preparations and radio would have played a vital role had anything gone wrong at the stroke of midnight, December 31, 1999. Besides, with the long weekend, the nearest local daily, the *Owen Sound Sun-Times*, wouldn't be publishing for two more days. Television, with its wide audience, was one other obvious option. But which TV station to use? How to be sure people would be watching the right channel? No. Radio was the best bet, McQuigge decided.

CKNX radio in Wingham, about thirty minutes from Walkerton, first broadcast to the public in 1926, though its initials dated from 1935. In the late 1930s, towns around the area clamoured to host NX's Saturday-night live "Barn Dance" broadcast. Radio had begun a swift ascent as the primary conduit for fast-breaking news against which no newspaper could compete. Even to this day, almost two-thirds of people in Bruce County twelve years and older tune in to CKNX at some point during the week. Still, it's fair to say, the latter half of the 1900s were not exactly kind to Canadian radio's newsgathering operations, especially those at smaller stations. Reporting staffs were either pared to the bone or eliminated. With rare, mostly big-city exceptions, private radio newsrooms go unstaffed after-hours and on weekends. Just about the only live radio news Canadians get in off-hours comes from Broadcast News in Toronto, a subsidiary off The Canadian Press, the country's national news agency. But CKNX does have someone in its newsroom during parts of the weekend. Coming in before five that morning, Gord Dougan had found two messages on the station's answering machine. Both appeared to be from the same person and both had come in sometime Saturday evening or overnight.

"You better do something," the caller said. "There's something wrong with our water supply up here in Walkerton. I think there's contamination."

Dougan didn't know what to make of it. Was it a hoax? The best way to find out, he figured, was to call the medical officer of health. He waited until a more reasonable hour, reaching McQuigge at home at about 9:30 A.M. Did the doctor know of any problems with Walkerton's water? Could there be a link to the previous week's floods?

"The water supply for Walkerton is from a deep well so it should be secure. It shouldn't be subject to any contamination," McQuigge told him, adding that the incubation period for gastric illness would suggest the problem predated the floods.

McQuigge went on to say that one hundred people had phoned the town's hospital, two dozen had shown up with symptoms of diarrhea and cramps, and one stool sample had tested positive for E. coli. In addition, two children were in hospital in Owen Sound for observation. The health unit was doing its own tests. He promised to call as soon as he had any further information. At 11 A.M., Dougan began his newscast with this understated opening:

"A number of people in the Walkerton area are not having the best of long holiday weekends. The Walkerton hospital has received about one hundred calls from people suffering from diarrhea."

Dougan reported McQuigge's comments and repeated the information on the noon newscast. He then left for the day, leaving the newsroom unstaffed. When McQuigge called minutes later to inform the station of the boil-water advisory, he got voicemail. Undaunted, he left a message saying he was putting out the warning and was heading to his office in Owen Sound. Then, not realizing it was the Environment Ministry he was calling, he contacted the Spills Action Centre in Toronto to ask for an emergency number for the province's public health branch. Paul Webb, who took the call, laughed aloud when McQuigge said he was investigating an E. coli outbreak in Walkerton. But after checking with someone, he told McQuigge the hotline had received an anonymous call a day earlier.

"We know they're working on the drinking water lines up there," said Webb.

"We knew that too, but the PUC there is telling us that everything is fine," McQuigge replied.

"That's what we were told too."

Webb then told McQuigge that the Spills Action Centre had tracked down a John Koebel, the manager of Walkerton's PUC, who'd reported "minimum adverse sampling" in the system.

"Well, we're really into something," McQuigge said grimly. "We've got over one hundred and twenty cases of something and we think it's E. coli bloody diarrhea."

"Oh jeez."

Hundreds more people might have drunk Walkerton's poisonous water had not McQuigge's voicemail to CKNX triggered a pager carried by reporter Scott Pettigrew. He immediately headed to the station and, based on the voicemail, quickly wrote the 2 P.M. newscast.

Sunday, May 21
2 P.M.

"The Bruce-Grey-Owen Sound Health Unit has issued a boil-water advisory for all Walkerton residents. Medical Officer of Health Dr. Murray McQuigge says close to one hundred people have called the Walkerton hospital complaining of diarrhea. Two children were sick enough to have been transferred to the Grey-Bruce Regional Health Centre in Owen Sound," Pettigrew read on-air.

"Again, the Bruce-Grey-Owen Sound Health Unit is asking all Walkerton residents to boil water before being used for drinking and cooking."

The advisory topped the news for the next several hours. By the end of the day, close to half of everyone in Walkerton had heard about it. Of those, almost one-third had heard it on the radio. A higher percentage heard about it through word of mouth. But more than half the population remained blissfully unaware of the warning to avoid the lethally contaminated water flowing from their taps. Moreover, in an inexplicable oversight, the health unit failed to notify the Walkerton hospital, which began moving to bottled water only as nurses on shift change or patients spread the word. It would also take two more days before Maple Court Villa and Brucelea Haven, homes to some of the town's most at-risk residents, or the jail were formally notified. Still, what had begun as a low-key announcement on a local radio station was on its way to becoming one of the country's biggest news stories.

For Peter and Esther Raymond, the news was desperate. Their toddler's condition had taken a sharp turn for the worse. The bloody diarrhea persisted. She threw up constantly. She cried as painful cramps convulsed her. Her delicate face was becoming puffy. It was time to fly her to London. The next flight she would make would be to the East Coast for burial.

David Patterson heard the boil-water advisory he'd so recently crafted on the car radio as he made the twenty-minute drive from his home in Tara to the Owen Sound office. He'd been all but consumed by the crisis for two days now, and he struggled to make sense of it. He bounded up the stairs into the office, clutching his handwritten copy of the advisory, which he handed to Mary Sellars to type up and fax to the newspapers. Patterson then picked up the phone and called Stan Koebel, who had spent another three hours that morning flushing the system.

"Just want to let you know that we've issued a boil-water advisory for Walkerton," Patterson told him.

There was a brief silence.

"I wish you'd called me before you'd done that," Stan replied.

"We had no choice, Stan. You know. We can't figure out anything else but the water."

Stan told Patterson he'd been flushing at Mother Teresa school for sixteen hours and that chlorine levels were high.

"Any suggestions about what else we should be doing?"

Patterson considered. This wasn't his area of expertise. But he told Stan it made sense to be raising the chlorine levels. He then headed to the boardroom for the first of what would become dozens of such gatherings aimed at controlling what was now clearly an epidemic. Life for the members of the health unit had been turned upside down, but Stan Koebel's universe was disintegrating. He sought refuge in a reassuring routine: cutting the grass in the yard behind his home. Surely, if he went about his normal business, did as he always did, just pretended nothing was wrong, the growing sense of doom would go away? But the mental ramparts he was trying so desperately to build as a buttress against reality stood no chance.

Sunday, May 21
2:57 P.M.

"Is John there please?" the caller asked.

"*John?*"

"Koebel."

"You must have the wrong number. I don't know a *John* Koebel," Stan's wife responded.

Chris Johnson was puzzled.

"I was given this number by the manager of the public utilities commission. I'm with the Ministry of the Environment."

"Oh, it's *Stan* Koebel," said Carole.

"Okay. This is *Stan* Koebel's residence?"

"Yep. And he's the manager of the PUC."

"*Stan* is?"

"Yes."

"Okay. Then what's *John?*"

"I don't know who *John* Koebel is. It was his uncle that's dead," said Carole with a chuckle.

"Is *Stan* in?"

"Ah yeah, he's just cutting the grass."

Carole went out and called her husband. He turned off the mower. The sweat showed under his arms and on his flushed, furrowed brow.

"Hi, Stan, it's the Ministry of the Environment Spills Action Centre calling. I'm sorry to bother you. We've had the adverse water samples in the Walkerton water distribution system and the possible E. coli cases."

Stan still couldn't quite figure out exactly who the caller was, even though he'd spoken to him a day earlier.

"You said there had been minimal adverse sampling in the past. Do you have any record of that?"

"Two weeks ago. I haven't sampled for this week yet."

Stan was lying and he knew it. How could he admit that he'd known for days about the results of the samples he'd taken less than a week earlier? Why even mention it when he'd heard nothing from the ministry people in Owen Sound? Surely they'd have called if there had been a problem.

"So you'll be doing sampling on Tuesday then?"

"Oh yeah," he answered confidently. "Yes."

This was a far more comfortable area of conversation. Stan was sure the next samples would come up clean. They had to, given that they would be taken after almost three days of flushing and overdosing the system on chlorine. What else could he possibly do? He'd even called his counterpart in Wingham for advice, mentioning only the reports of illness but not the bad lab results.

"We're flushing and superchlorinating," he said. "Is that the right thing or not?"

"That's all you can do."

Stan figured he'd better call Mayor Dave Thomson to check whether he'd heard about the boil-water advisory. Yes, Thomson said. Dr. McQuigge had told him. To Stan's relief, the mayor didn't seem too concerned. For the first time in three days, the exhausted water manager began to believe the situation was under control. He couldn't have been more wrong.

Sunday, May 21
5 P.M.

After the second strategy meeting of the afternoon, Patterson heard from John Alden of the London public-health lab, whom he'd paged earlier. Alden, who was at home, listened as Patterson explained the pressing nature of the situation and the health unit's suspicion that the water in Walkerton was contaminated with E. coli O157. He offered to meet Patterson at the lab to get

tests started immediately. With that arranged, Patterson called
James Schmidt and asked him to collect water samples in
Walkerton. Restaurants would probably be the best bet because
they'd be open. In addition, he asked Schmidt to get samples
from the health unit office and the hospital itself.

"About twenty samples is what we need. I'll come down to
Walkerton right away to pick them up and take them myself to
London," Patterson said, ignoring McQuigge's advice to send
them down by taxi.

Patterson called two other members of the health unit at home
and asked them to report to work the following day, the Victoria
Day public holiday. He then set out for Walkerton. It was well after
8 P.M. when he stopped by Brucelea Haven to pick up the stool
samples they'd stashed in the fridge. He then met up with
Schmidt, who passed on the water samples he had gathered from
the town's taps. There was one more stop to make: Maple Court
Villa nursing home, where Patterson picked up more stool samples
and some vials of the water as well. At neither place did he remember to mention the boil-water advisory.

Sunday, May 21
8:30 P.M.

A blood-curdling scream pierced the Sunday-evening calm of the
McDonald home, a sound that will always stay with Jamie. He
bounded downstairs to find five-year-old Ian doubled over in
agony. He bundled the child into the car and drove the few
hundred metres to the hospital, where about twenty or thirty
people, a cross-section of the community, filled emergency. All
looked pale and miserable and hunched over. Dr. David Barr
examined Ian and told his worried dad to keep him hydrated with
bottled water.

"This is going to be Third World Mexico for the next few
weeks," Barr told a disbelieving McDonald.

Sunday, May 21
10 P.M.

Dave Patterson had barely begun the two-hundred-kilometre drive to the laboratory in London when his supervisor called him en route to tell him that little Mary Rose Raymond was in critical care. Patterson wanted to cry. When Murray McQuigge heard the same news, he began to wonder whether there would even be enough dialysis machines in the province to look after an expected deluge of hemolytic uremic syndrome. The concern abated when he heard that evening about peritoneal dialysis, a method by which fluid is pumped through the child's abdomen to flush out the toxins. Patterson arrived in London well after midnight and called John Alden at home. Alden promptly joined him at the lab to take possession of the water samples and get the analysis started. It was after 3 A.M. when Patterson made it back home to Tara, having almost run into a deer on the way.

11

Death on a Holiday

Victoria Day, Monday, May 22
7:30 A.M.

D AVE AND CAROLYN BIESENTHAL had raised four kids, two
boys and two girls, in their quiet corner of Bruce County.
One of them, Laryssa, had put Walkerton on the international
map in a way that had made an entire town swell with pride. As
part of Canada's Olympic rowing team, she had brought home a
coveted bronze medal from the 1996 Olympics in Atlanta. Not
shabby for a homegrown girl from a little Ontario town, which considered it as good as gold and threw a huge parade in her honour.
But no matter where else she lived or travelled, Stonegate farm was
always home and the long weekend in May found her there for
some rest and relaxation. With her were six friends from the
rowing team that was preparing for the 2000 Games in Sydney
still a few months off. It didn't get much better than this when it
came to comfortable peace and quiet. A contented hush fell over
the countryside on the holiday Monday. But that hush was rudely

smashed by the jolting mechanical roar of helicopters coming and going at the local hospital a few short kilometres to the east.

"There must have been one helluva car accident somewhere," Dave said to Carolyn.

Hours and days were starting to blur for Dave Patterson. The issuance of the boil-water advisory the previous afternoon had only thrown the health unit into more frantic activity and he'd managed to get just a few hours of sleep for a second straight night. It wasn't quite 8 A.M. when he asked James Schmidt to collect a second set of water samples in Walkerton and get them to London. The health unit outbreak team had been scheduled to assemble at about 2 P.M., but Dr. McQuigge called everybody in to Owen Sound early. The team scrambled to the office. McQuigge started the meeting at 10 A.M. Patterson hurried in about an hour later, missing the recap of the events of the past few days that he already knew well. McQuigge's own morning had been occupied with an unending series of phone calls with other health officials, hospitals, doctors, laboratories. McQuigge had also talked to several local radio and TV reporters looking for information on the outbreak. He used the opportunities to get the message out about how to avoid secondary cases, those in which caregivers become infected. Shortly before 1 P.M., McQuigge heard from local Environment Ministry supervisor Phil Bye, whom the health unit had alerted earlier in the day. McQuigge impressed upon Bye the magnitude of the epidemic and the need for an immediate investigation. Bye, who two years earlier had overruled Michelle Zillinger's recommendation to take legal action against the Walkerton Public Utilities Commission, promised to send in one of his officers right away.

Victoria Day, Monday, May 22
12:55 P.M.

John Earl was at home when the Spills Action Centre in Toronto phoned to ask him to respond to an incident of adverse water quality and disease outbreak in Walkerton. Earl had been with the Environment Ministry for a quarter-century. Following his degree in environmental studies in 1974, he'd joined the regional office in Owen Sound and never left. Over the years, he'd drifted up through the ranks to the position of senior environmental abatement officer, working mostly on the industrial side. In April 1999, he assumed responsibility for communal water though he had never had any training on water-related issues. His first contact with the Walkerton PUC occurred a few months later, when the testing laboratory, GAP, sent along results of samples that showed bacteria in the town's water, specifically E. coli. Earl didn't grasp the significance. He didn't follow up. Nor did he know he was supposed to forward the results to the public health unit. Like so many others, he'd never heard of E. coli O157 and had no idea it could kill. A few months later, a second set of adverse samples arrived in his office, but Earl was on vacation and a colleague forgot to tell him about them. In October 1999, Earl was temporarily shipped back over to the industrial inspection program. Larry Struthers, another long-time and equally untrained member of the Owen Sound office, took over communal water for six months. On April 12, 2000, Struthers handed the responsibility back to Earl. The two men talked about outstanding issues for two hours, but Walkerton didn't come up. In all, the ministry received seven faxes in April indicating that there was bad water in Walkerton, but any alarm bells had been muffled by bureaucratic ineptitude, complacency, fuzzy guidelines, and a general antipathy toward aggressive action. Besides, municipal water systems took up just a tiny fraction of the ministry's time. It was, as the highest-level ministry managers had decided, a non-priority.

Earl headed to the office, arriving about an hour later. He contacted Dave Patterson, who informed him of the alarming number of cases of gastric disease, likely due to E. coli O157.

"We've run out of options," Patterson said by way of explanation for the day-old boil-water advisory.

"What do you need from me?" Earl asked.

"We need you to get all bacteriological sampling results in the past two weeks, records of flows, records of chlorine residuals, and any other potentially useful information on the water there," Patterson replied.

"We also need any documentation regarding the construction and disinfection of water mains. Oh yeah, find out whether the operating authorities knew of any unusual events in the past two weeks. You should be able to get all the information from the manager, Stan Koebel."

Earl scanned a faxed report of the calls to the Spills Action Centre and jotted down a few notes in his almost illegible handwriting.

"Situation started on Friday. Illness in Walkerton. Bloody diarrhea. Two hundred calls. One hundred people entering in three hospitals. Using unlicensed operators at the water system."

Earl talked to Phil Bye, who asked him to get a map of the water distribution system in Walkerton and to find the most recent ministry inspection reports. He then called Stan Koebel to say he'd be down within the hour. He noted the various pieces of information he wanted and asked him to have them ready for his arrival. It was a call Stan had been dreading. Although it was only early afternoon, he felt exhausted after another morning of running around and flushing hydrants. At times, it felt as if he were moving through molasses. For what felt like the hundredth time in several days, he drove down Yonge Street, past the Becker's and Valu-Mart, and turned right at the corner across the road from Walkerton District Secondary School onto Highway 9. He drove up the hill, Mel's Diner and Saugeen Filter Supply on the right, the Energizer plant on the left, past the visitor centre that featured a large poster of Laryssa Biesenthal in her rowing shell and the road leading to the PUC shop, down the dip past Percy Pletsch's old farm and Stonegate, and turned right at the second mile-and-a-quarter. A few minutes later, Stan pulled up at the small cement-block pumphouse that housed Well 7. He felt sick. The daily log sheet was a mess. Earl would immediately know something was wrong. He left the sheet there, fetched the ones

from the other wells, and went back to the office to await the
unwelcome visitor.

As Earl drove down to Walkerton, it occurred to him that the
anonymous caller had detailed information about the town's system.
He wondered if someone had deliberately poisoned the water.

Victoria Day, Monday, May 22
2 P.M.

Despite the brightness of the day, the grey offices that were home
to the health unit were bustling in a gloom the fluorescent lighting couldn't quite dispel. Telephones rang constantly. People
clutching notepads scurried up and down the stairs rather than
wait for the old, slow elevator. There were hurried conversations,
meetings, more scurrying, more meetings. The health unit was
moving into crisis mode. Some tracked patients. Others offered
advice to doctors on the best treatment for E. coli poisoning and
on what signs might herald kidney distress or failure. New information was posted on the unit's Web site, which saw the number
of queries start a steep climb from the usual one-thousand hits
per day to thirty thousand. Copies of the boil-water advisory were
faxed to the local newspapers. Literature was prepared so other
staff could start work the following day with all the information
at their fingertips. In mid-afternoon, James Schmidt called to say
he'd collected a second set of water samples and delivered them
to the lab in London. Dave Patterson instructed him to repeat
the entire process yet again the following day. In addition, he told
Schmidt to deliver a series of notices on E. coli and preventing
its spread to all food premises in Walkerton.

The health unit had now gathered information sheets on 120
patients, which were divvied up among the team members. They
analysed the data, paying special attention to the onset of the
illness and to where patients lived. McQuigge took it upon
himself to call the parents of every child under five he knew to
have diarrhea, about fifteen in all.

"You Ian's father? This is Dr. McQuigge. I'm quite certain Ian has E. coli."

Jamie McDonald didn't need convincing. He and Cathy had watched their boy scream as waves of excruciating cramps racked his frame. After listening to McQuigge outline the signs of kidney failure, McDonald took Ian back to the Walkerton emergency department. They bumped into an obviously distressed neighbour, Bob McKay, as they left home. There were fifty people in emergency. McDonald could hardly believe it. Staff took blood from Ian and told them to go home.

Victoria Day, Monday, May 22
4 P.M.

By the time John Earl arrived at the PUC office, Stan Koebel had already pulled together most of the information he'd been asked to collect. Stan struck Earl as tired, even a little distraught. The manager was cooperative, although he didn't volunteer much information beyond what he was asked for. He dutifully produced a map of the system along with some handwritten notes on chlorine residuals. He provided two lab reports, both dated May 5, which indicated bacterial contamination in both raw and treated water from Well 5. He also produced the lab report that A&L had faxed to the PUC the previous Wednesday, the one he'd essentially ignored for several days, the one showing the town's tap water to be heavily contaminated with both bacteria and E. coli. Earl glanced at it, but the astonishing information didn't register. Had he looked more closely, he might also have realized it contained a startling anomaly: the treated water showed as grossly contaminated while the raw water had tested clean. And had he scoured the daily operating sheets of the wells Stan handed him, he'd have noticed a consistent pattern of chlorine residuals that might have immediately inspired suspicion. He stuffed the paperwork into his briefcase.

"I don't know what, if anything, is wrong," Stan was saying.

"Has there been anything unusual you can think of in the last couple of weeks?"

"Well, we took Well 6 out of service due to a lightning strike that damaged one of the control switches for the pumphouse. Other than that, no, can't think of anything."

Earl remembered the note in the action centre's report and asked about the qualifications of the operators. Stan responded that he and Frank were the chief operators and were properly certified, although he conceded they occasionally used another employee who was not.

"You had any problems with your staff?" Earl asked.

Stan didn't answer directly. Instead, he talked about the possibility of the municipality taking over operation of the water system. That had created some uncertainty, he said. He also mentioned, without elaboration, that one of the guys had been off work for some time. In any event, Stan assured him, there was no reason to suspect any intentional damage or deliberate contamination of the water system. He also talked about the vicious May 12 storm, and they discussed whether it could have affected the wells. Stan explained that Well 7 was an artesian well in which the water naturally bubbled upwards when the pump was shut off. The well had an overflow pipe. That, said Stan, was the only way surface water could have entered the system. Earl collected a water sample at the PUC office and two more at Well 7. He asked Stan to get any reports or documentation from the construction firms involved in the new mains. Stan agreed. Earl said he'd return the next morning to pick them up and drove back to the Owen Sound office, while Stan went to his daughter's place to continue filling her swimming pool. At the office, Earl dropped off the samples he'd taken, along with the other information Stan had provided and went home. Despite the urgency of the situation, he didn't call David Patterson, who was anxiously awaiting any information, such as the previous week's test results.

On the six o'clock news, a worried mother in the Walkerton emergency waiting room gently rubbed the bare chest and tummy of her dull-eyed tyke sitting on her lap. For the first time, the boil-water advisory had made it to TV, along with the PUC's contention that the water was safe.

Victoria Day, Monday, May 22
6:30 P.M.

The members of the health-unit outbreak team gathered again in the "war room." From the line charts and information provided by doctors and hospitals, they plotted an epidemiological curve showing that the peak of the onset of symptoms had occurred on May 17, the previous Wednesday, the day A&L labs had faxed Stan the results showing contamination of the drinking water. Working backwards, they calculated the infections would most likely have occurred the previous Friday, May 12, possibly a day or two later. With that done, each member of the team called out the addresses of the patients from their share of the line listings. As each address was named, Patterson used a yellow marker to highlight a large map of Walkerton he'd pinned up on one wall. By the end of the exercise, the entire map was covered in yellow.

"It can only be the water," someone said, and everyone nodded.

A world away in the London hospital to which she'd been airlifted from Walkerton just hours earlier, sixty-six-year-old Lenore Al, a retired library worker who was suffering from cancer, passed away. She left her husband, three sons, and ten grandchildren. It had been just four days since she'd shown the first symptoms of E. coli poisoning. In the critical care unit, Mary Rose Raymond was showing some signs of improvement. In Walkerton, eighty-four-year-old Laura Rowe had been admitted to hospital with diarrhea. Her already weak heart would stop beating a week later.

12

Ripping the Veil

Tuesday, May 23
7:30 A.M.

THE FIRST DAY of the shortened workweek saw Stan Koebel arrive at the PUC shop even earlier than was his usual practice. The others could immediately tell he was anxious, upset, exhausted. For one thing, he was smoking. Stan never smoked. He and Frank talked about the boil-water advisory. Frank had heard it on Sunday but chose to ignore it.

"We got to get out and do some flushing," Stan said. "I've already jacked up the chlorine out at 7."

Stan was probably just overreacting again. But that was Stan: always serious, always anxious. And yet Frank, too, was starting to feel nervous, perhaps more so than he cared to admit. Something was different this time.

"You've got a lot of work to do today," he said to Al Buckle and the other guys. "Get out and start flushing every hydrant in town."

As the others left, Stan turned to Frank.

"The ministry guy is coming back," he said quietly. "Go to Well 7 and get the operating sheet. You know, make it presentable."

Tuesday, May 23
8:45 A.M.

From the laboratory in London, John Alden called Dave Patterson to tell him the twenty samples he had hand-delivered on Sunday were showing high bacterial counts, including E. coli. Tests on the Monday samples were also showing early signs of similar serious contamination. Patterson was shocked. Disbelieving. Everything he'd ever learned, ever experienced, told him that as long as there's chlorine in the system, bacteria can't survive.

Patterson hung up and called ministry supervisor Phil Bye.

"Something has definitely gone wrong with the Walkerton water system," said Patterson.

The unfolding crisis was slowly starting to filter through to the province's politicians. The Ministry of Health called looking for details. A political aide in Toronto asked for information that could be passed on to the health minister. The first sparks of what would become a political firestorm had been ignited. It was time to go back to the source.

"Stan, our tests have come back," Patterson said. "The water is bad."

There was no response.

"When were the last bacteriological tests that you took?"

A few moments passed.

"A week ago Monday," came the reply.

"And the results?"

Again, there was a silence that seemed to last for minutes.

"They all failed, but I just found them on Saturday, on my desk."

There was another long silence, then a muffled sobbing.

"I can't believe it, Stan," Patterson said, his disappointment barely disguised. "How can this be?"

Patterson listened in stunned amazement as Stan talked about the PUC's recent change in laboratories.

"We might have a communication problem with the new company," he said, and he began to cry.

"It's okay, Stan," Patterson soothed. "Have there been any other recent changes?"

"I've been changing the chlorinator."

"Does that mean there's been a lapse in chlorination?"

"Well, it wasn't working properly, you know, on and off, so that's why I changed it."

Patterson scribbled down notes as Stan talked.

"What should we do?" Stan asked, his voice tinged with despair. After all, days of superchlorination had raised the levels of chlorine in the water. Patterson didn't respond immediately.

"Let me ask you, Stan. Do you have any idea of what might have happened here?"

Stan considered. It had to be Well 7. He explained how the level rises in the artesian well when it's not pumping. The overflow is discharged into a nearby swamp that may have flooded with the recent heavy rains. When the well's pump had come on, it might have sucked the swamp water back in through the pipe, which only had a flimsy flap on it designed to keep out animals and birds. Stan had once described the flap as Mickey Mouse, but it had been there from Day 1 and the Environment Ministry had approved it.

"Did you explain this to John Earl?"

"Yeah, I talked to John," Stan replied.

"Who do you report to?"

"The PUC commission."

"Look, Stan, you'd better tell them. You've got to be honest."

"Yeah," came the murmured response.

The line went quiet and Stan began sobbing again, more loudly this time, more persistently.

"I'm not sleeping. We're running on a shoestring," he wailed. "Not enough dedicated people. We should have one person dedicated just to the water. I've been telling them this for years."

"Oh my God, Stan."

His mind a jumble, Patterson grabbed his notes and raced to McQuigge's office.

"It's the water!" he said. "The lab tests show it's the water." Stan put the phone down on his desk and slumped forward in his chair, his face red, his eyes strained and puffy from lack of sleep.

"Oh my God, it's the water," he said to Janice Hallahan. "The samples have come back and it's the water."

It felt as if a devastating earthquake had rumbled through his world. For twenty-eight years he had helped run the utilities commission. For twenty-eight years, the lights had stayed on and the water had been just fine. How could this be? He'd fought so hard, so valiantly, to deal with the situation. He'd flushed and increased the chlorine. What else could he have done? But it had all come to naught. Everything he'd tried to do had failed. His entire world was set to come crashing down and he knew it. He buried his face in his hands. To the casual visitor, the large bookcase filled from floor to ceiling with books and binders lent an air of authority and technical competence to the man who'd occupied the office for the past twelve years. Now they bore only mute witness to the inadequacy of a man charged with the safety of a water system that fed five thousand unsuspecting people.

"Better call the insurance company to let them know," he at last said to Hallahan. "We could have some liability on our hands."

At the top of the long driveway and inside the horse clinic that Dr. David Biesenthal ran three times a week, a horse's owner was speculating that a water main had broken and sewage had gotten into the town's drinking water. That might account for the dew-worm smell Carolyn had complained about, Biesenthal rejoined. The clinic phone rang and Carolyn answered. It was her daughter-in-law, Kim, whose children were in a Walkerton day care while she worked in the office of Dr. Susan McArthur, the physician who had initially treated Mary Rose Raymond.

"Please get our kids out of town," she said to a startled Carolyn. "There are people out there dying. It's worse than you think."

In Owen Sound, Murray McQuigge remained grimly silent as Dave Patterson, his voice wavering, recounted briefly the conversation he'd just had with Stan Koebel.

"We'd better head to Walkerton," McQuigge announced. "I'll call Mayor Thomson and let him know we're coming."

Patterson scurried to alert other members of the team.

"Dave, we've got a terrible situation on our hands," McQuigge told the mayor. "Our tests show the water is grossly contaminated."

He relayed Patterson's conversation with Stan. Thomson remained curiously quiet.

"You may want to get someone down to Stan. He sounds suicidal. You know, just to keep an eye on him. And you'd better get a council meeting together. Make it 2 P.M."

Thomson thought for a few moments before suggesting they meet at Newman's, the restaurant located in the landmark Hartley House hotel on the corner of Durham and Jackson. It's a short block from council chambers and a traditional meeting place for local businessmen and politicians alike. McQuigge didn't think it the greatest place to meet but let it slide. Five members of the health unit piled into the car and headed for Walkerton. Mary Sellars, McQuigge's secretary, took notes as they drove. Patterson borrowed McQuigge's cellphone and alerted Phil Bye to the meeting. The rest of the trip was taken up with strategizing how best to present what they knew to council and what information they needed to pass on to the medical community.

Tuesday, May 23
11:30 A.M.

The first event for the team was a joint news conference with the Walkerton hospital set up by Dianne Waram, the hospital's acting administrator. The steady trickle of media calls had grown into a raging torrent that was threatening to swamp them. Better one large news conference than to have to deal with dozens of individual reporters. Besides, it was urgent to impress on the town just how bad the situation was and what measures to take to prevent it from getting worse. With the news conference out of the way, the team gathered in the hospital cafeteria for a quick bite to eat, then met half-a-dozen local doctors in the boardroom, with another taking part by teleconference call. McQuigge gave advice on how to look for and treat cases of E. coli O157–induced kidney failure in children and how to avoid secondary cases, the most effective means being a thorough handwashing. The meeting finished shortly after 1:30 P.M. The outbreak team piled back into the car and headed for Newman's.

Tuesday, May 23
1:45 P.M.

As they entered the restaurant where Mayor Dave Thomson and his councillors were gathered, ministry supervisor Phil Bye took McQuigge and Patterson aside. He motioned them into "the library," a room off the lobby filled with surplus books from the public library down the street. Bye was tense. He told them the ministry's enforcement branch was investigating and they planned to issue legal orders to the town. Patterson and McQuigge nodded in agreement and the trio headed into the restaurant, where Thomson and his councillors were ordering lunch. Patterson and McQuigge, who had been fretting all morning about the choice of location, bridled.

"This isn't an appropriate place to have this kind of conversation," Patterson said to the nonplussed politicians. "Can we go to council offices?"

"We've just ordered lunch," Thomson protested.

"Well then you'd better cancel," McQuigge growled. The outbreak team turned and headed for the doors.

"Guess we'd better go," Thomson remarked as the others disappeared from view.

The mayor and his deputy, Councillor Rolly Anstett, headed into the kitchen and apologized for having to bolt. Just send the bill, Thomson said. They trooped out of the restaurant and made the quick walk to the municipal office. Inside, the members of the health unit passed a drinking water fountain.

"There should be a sign on that fountain," McQuigge said to the women behind the counter.

The admonition was met with laughter. McQuigge fumed. He stalked into the council chambers, where the student-like desks were quickly rearranged. They all sat down under the smiling gaze of a young Queen Elizabeth, her portrait snug against the bare beige-toned concrete block wall. McQuigge opened the meeting by emphasizing the seriousness of the situation, the high incidence of illness, the possibility of deaths. He was obviously angry, and appeared to be struggling to control himself. Everyone listened intently as he spoke. Above the Queen, the plastic clock with the square gold-coloured frame ticked away the minutes. And sitting there silently, barely moving, was Stan Koebel, his face flushed, his head bowed.

"The ministry is going to be ordering immediate action," Bye said. "I should also warn you that charges could be laid."

Councillors discussed how best to disseminate information on the boil-water advisory and about E. coli. The post office is next door, someone noted. Perhaps they could drop the information directly into everyone's mailboxes.

"We have some questions," Thomson said, turning to McQuigge.

"Could the public have been made aware of this earlier?"

McQuigge's blood pressure rose another notch. He reviewed the unit's actions, starting with Dr. Kristen Hallett's call, and how they had tracked the increasing number of cases through the weekend, culminating in the boil-water advisory on the Sunday.

And then McQuigge was asked if the boil-water advisory could have been better advertised.

"I called the mayor and I called the radio stations, so everyone knew by Sunday afternoon," he said emphatically.

"Was the holiday a factor?" a councillor asked.

McQuigge shook his head and walked the meeting through how he and his staff had spent days investigating the epidemic.

"We went at this hammer and tong all long weekend," he pronounced.

It was too much for Patterson. The quiet, self-contained man was furious at the last question. How dare they? He had worked almost non-stop since Friday. He had raced to London in the middle of the night with water samples, almost killing a deer and possibly himself on the way back. He had recommended putting out the boil-water advisory and had drawn it up despite the uncertainties, despite Stan's assurances. It was through his efforts and those of his colleagues that they'd traced the epidemic to the water. How dare anyone even suggest they'd all spent the long weekend goofing off while people were getting sick and dying?

"Stan, do you have anything to add at this point?" asked McQuigge, who found it surprising the PUC manager was even present given what he'd heard earlier about his state of mind.

Everyone turned to Stan Koebel, who briefly met their gaze before staring down at his clasped hands. He cleared his throat and began to talk about the new main construction on Highway 9 and the problems they'd had with it, interjecting quickly that it wasn't connected to the system. But he made no mention of what he'd told Dave Patterson: that he'd had the bad lab results for days, that the chlorinator had been out of service. McQuigge could stand it no more.

"Come on, Stan," he interrupted loudly, angrily. "Come on, Stan, come clean."

Stan looked stunned. Thomson flinched. The room was quiet. They all stared at Stan, who seemed to be shrinking before their eyes.

"Didn't you have a fax last Thursday showing your water was contaminated?" McQuigge asked.

"Yes," came the almost inaudible response.

"And what were the results of those samples?"

"They all failed."

"And didn't you tell Dave Patterson that you had a chlorinator that hadn't worked for some time?"

"Yes."

A thick, heavy silence descended on the room. Someone let out a long, low whistle. Stan covered his face with his hands and began sobbing quietly.

"Why did you assure us the water was safe if the chlorinator wasn't working?" McQuigge demanded.

"I believed we had good quality water, and assurances from Frank and myself," he pleaded. "We thought we were flushing and chlorinating as a precautionary measure, to make sure it wasn't the water."

He took a deep breath before trying to explain further: the chlorination from Well 6 should have been sufficient to disinfect the system, even though the unit at Well 7 wasn't working. The rationale seemed to make perfect sense. Years ago, unchlorinated water from Well 1 was disinfected as it mixed with treated water from Well 2. He talked about the overflow pipe at Well 7. The swamp in which the well was located might have flooded from the big storm and dirty water might have made its way through the flimsy flap and into the well.

"Look, we don't know what's happened here," Bye began. "We have a number of situations that have to be addressed. Maybe it's Well 7, maybe it's the replacement of the mains."

"That's not possible," Stan protested quietly, his voice breaking. "That can't be."

He was completely exhausted, befuddled. Bye threw out more possibilities.

"Maybe there's problems with cross-connections or maybe there's inadequate chlorination."

His desperation clearly evident, Stan asked what he should do. It wasn't the ministry's job to offer that kind of advice, Bye responded. Get a consultant, he said.

A furious McQuigge was hardly paying attention. But if the doctor was angry, so was Thomson, who throughout the meeting had been struggling to grasp it all. McQuigge's loud voice and accusatory tone bothered him intensely. It was as if he were trying to force Stan into making some kind of confession when he obviously didn't have a clue. How dare he lay into Stan under the circumstances? How unprofessional! First he says the man is suicidal, then he attacks him, humiliates him, hangs him out to dry in front of all these people. The clock above the Queen ticked relentlessly.

"Think we'd better leave now," McQuigge said to his team. The light bulb had gone on for McQuigge. They're going to blame the health unit for not acting more quickly. That, he decided, would never be allowed to happen. As he rose from his desk, McQuigge leaned toward Thomson and motioned him toward the windows.

"Dave," he said. "Now's the time to tell the public what you know."

"Yes, you've already told me that once," Thomson replied.

McQuigge was puzzled. He couldn't for the life of him recall having said anything like that to the mayor.

The human mind is a marvellous instrument. In a heartbeat, it synthesizes huge amounts of information, interprets the raw and disparate data provided by the senses to create a cohesive, meaningful whole. But at the same time, it is fallible as an objective chronicler of record because every cell of who we are is brought to bear on the incoming information. Our thoughts, our emotions, our biases act as filters, as prisms, as mirrors, especially in times of stress. Then, too, we are all capable of self-deception when the objective and subjective realities of our worlds, of ourselves, collide. So, we see what we want to see, hear what we want to hear. Often, we become implacably convinced of the truth of a self-invention. Perception, after all, is nine-tenths of reality. It is real because we believe it so. It is no lie because we believe it to be truth, and if others also believe it, if we make others believe it, then it must be true.

Thomson mulled over McQuigge's parting words. What was he getting at? Was it a threat? Didn't he say, "Don't you blow the whistle on me or else Brockton will . . . ?"

As he left the council offices, McQuigge noticed a Do Not Drink the Water sign had gone up over the drinking fountain. Similar signs had been going up in buildings all over the town. At the schools, water fountains and taps were shut down and covered over, bottled water brought in. People were advised to wash their hands with bleach amid rising fears about the disease spreading, especially among children.

Tuesday, May 23
3:30 P.M.

In the council chambers, the mood was grim. The first step, they decided, was to call Steve Burns, a consulting engineer who had studied the town's water system back in the early 1990s and was therefore familiar with it. They would try to set up a meeting with him for the morning. One of the councillors argued they should try to get Burns in that afternoon. A phone call confirmed that Burns was prepared to come immediately and on his arrival, council reconvened in a special session. Shortly after they began, Stan Koebel arrived and joined the discussion. Burns asked what he knew about the situation. In a monotone, Stan began by saying there had been some historical bacteria problems with Wells 5 and 7. At times he appeared confused, even disoriented. He'd looked at the A&L lab results showing the bad water the previous Thursday. One of the office girls had set the report on his desk. There had been complaints about too much chlorine in the water. He'd been flushing the system since Friday and was continuing to do so. When council suggested the town's works or volunteer fire department could help him out, he jumped at the offer. Burns said he'd have an action plan by morning.

"There's no magic to it," he said. "It's a matter of flushing, chlorinating, and taking samples."

To Stan it sounded exactly like what he'd been doing for so many hours over so many days.

In London, eighty-three-year-old Edith Pearson had already arrived from Walkerton after taking what would be the last trip of her life. Her family had lied that she had a heart condition to get the Walkerton hospital to admit her in the first place. In the critical-care unit, two-and-a-half-year-old Mary Raymond was losing her struggle. It had been just five days since she came down with a fever and diarrhea, just hours since she seemed to be getting better. But the E. coli poison had reached her brain, causing myriad tiny strokes. Her distraught mother held her tightly in her arms and clutched her to her breast as the unresponsive toddler quietly, imperceptibly, drew her last breath.

Around Walkerton, where poisonous water gushed from every hydrant in town, word of the two deaths began spreading from family to friends to neighbours to strangers. Anxiety and concern gave way to grief and panic and fear. What on earth was happening? Who's next? Slowly, the world was starting to notice. Reporters and photographers were arriving in droves. A small, sleepy town in Bruce County in midwestern Ontario was unwillingly, unwittingly, sliding to the top of the national news. It was as if a protective veil has been ripped aside, as if some giant invisible hand had swept the town into a strange dimension of darkness.

13

Blowing the Whistle

Wednesday, May 24
8:15 A.M.

A T WALKERTON DISTRICT Secondary School across the road from Mother Teresa, the day began with the usual playing of "O Canada," followed on this day by the Lord's Prayer. About eight hundred students attend the high school, seven hundred of whom bus or drive in from area towns and communities. The boil-water advisory had been in place for more than two full days now, but no one in Alex Cooper's Grade 10 geography class appeared to be perturbed. It seemed a little creepy, partly because no one had really explained what exactly the problem was, although Cooper had suggested before class that he thought it was E. coli.

"Omigod," someone said. "What's E. coli?"

The restless teenagers quieted as the announcement sounded over the intercom: the town's water had been contaminated and was unsafe to drink. The cause was unknown. There followed several minutes of detailed instructions on how to wash hands: put a blob of soap, which had mysteriously appeared in the normally empty washroom dispensers, in the middle of the palms and spread it outwards. Rinse off thoroughly, then use paper towels to close the taps. It seemed like the dumbest thing they'd ever heard. What's the point of using paper towels on the taps if they were washing their hands in contaminated water? Cooper told the class to wait and left. He returned a few minutes later.

"They hadn't thought that through," he said. "They're going to rethink it."

It was shortly before the lunch hour when the principal made another announcement.

"For your safety, we are going to send you home for the next two days while we sort this out."

"Yes!" A soft chorus arose from the class, fists punched the air, high-fives were exchanged. "Two days off!"

The teens streamed outside into the sunshine. They were greeted by the highly unusual sight of the yellow school buses waiting to take them home. Not even on the worst snow days are the buses brought in early. No matter, school was out for two days, and they busily chatted and made plans to get together. They had no idea they wouldn't see the inside of a classroom again for three weeks, that it would be almost four months before they'd be returning to their own school again, eight months before they could drink from the fountain. Nor did they know that in London, fellow 10th grader Jessica Crawford had just undergone emergency dialysis. When she was released from hospital three weeks later, her hands and arms were scarred from the 150 needles she'd had stuck in her, her stomach permanently etched by the dialysis.

Wednesday, May 24
11:58 A.M.

Frank Koebel was in the PUC shop at lunch hour when someone turned up the radio. Despite the boil-water advisory issued three days earlier, despite all the talk of illness, despite his brother's frantic flushing and insistence on raising the chlorine levels, the commotion still appeared somewhat abstract to him. He and his family had continued to drink the water. All this fuss and feathers was just that, he figured. Sure they'd usually try to flush the system each year in the spring but that was to get rid of rust and make sure the hydrants were working, not to get rid of bacteria. Sure, he'd heard on occasion about samples that suggested the possibility of bacteria in the water, but the resamples always came back clean, so the chances were that the bad ones were the result of contamination of the sampling bottles or taps. In any event, a little bacteria couldn't be that bad. Although Stan had never really shared the results of the inspection reports that revealed serious contamination problems, surely the ministry hotshots would have picked up on something serious enough to cause the kind of crisis unfolding around him. He stopped chewing as the news began:

"A baby and an elderly woman have died of an E. coli bacterial infection that has left hundreds ill in Walkerton, Ontario."

Frank Koebel's blood ran cold. A week later, he went to emergency with stomach cramps. He was given a muscle relaxant. He was also given a bottle for stool samples. He never used it.

Engineering consultant Steve Burns had arrived at council at about 8 A.M. that day with the action plan he'd spent much of the night preparing. The room was crowded: Janice Hallahan was on hand, as was Jim Kieffer, the PUC chairman. Also present was Ed Houghton, the manager of the utilities commission in Collingwood, which in 1996 had suffered through a six-month boil-water advisory after the parasite cryptosporidium was found in its drinking water. Stan Koebel was also there. He had just spent a couple of hours showing the system to Houghton, whom he'd asked the night before to come down to help out. Houghton discussed what the PUC had been doing. Stan stayed quiet. At some point, ministry supervisor Phil Bye showed up along with two of his superiors. The group talked about dumping all the highly chlorinated water from the two large towers and the threat that posed to the environment. They talked about Wells 6 and 7. Burns raised the possibility that a main might have been left open at the Highway 9 construction project causing the contamination.

"No, no, no," Stan protested and he began to weep. "That's not possible. The system was under pressure."

Terry Flynn of Frontline Corporate Communications joined the meeting, starting the meter ticking on a public-relations contract that would cost the town $46,000 a month, close to half a million dollars, by the time it was done. Flynn warned council to prepare for an onslaught of reporters demanding access and answers. The calls were already pouring in. Then someone came in and whispered something to the mayor no one there had heard before: People had died. There was a stunned silence. It seemed as if Stan Koebel would explode.

Three people had now died: Lenore Al, Mary Rose Raymond, and Edith Pearson, who passed away in a morphine haze in London as her family watched helplessly. It had been just four days since the Walkerton emergency room had sent her home with the standard recommendation to drink plenty of fluids. In Owen Sound, the phones in the health unit's head office rang off the hook. It was the same situation at its smaller branch offices. Among the many calls, there were pointed questions. How on earth did this happen? Gradually, it seemed, the questions were shifting to accusations. You people knew there was diarrhea. What took you so long?

Fiercely proud as he was of his organization and the way it had responded to the outbreak, the mere suggestion that the health unit had mishandled the situation rankled McQuigge. Still, he felt certain that Mayor Thomson would tell the public what he'd heard from Stan Koebel. Surely, McQuigge said to Patterson, the mayor would use a news conference to mention the information, or rather misinformation, Stan had provided the health unit during its initial frantic search for the cause of the epidemic. Better a day late than never.

Dave Thomson was both nervous and unhappy. He had no desire to hang Stan out to dry, certainly not at McQuigge's behest. His blood boiled every time he thought back to how the bull-headed McQuigge had gone after Stan. Where was the compassion? The mercy? Everything about that confrontation, more like an ambush, a sniper attack, was wrong. What was the point of the iron fist? Stan couldn't have been expected to defend himself under the circumstances, what with a ministry investigation underway and possible charges coming down the road and all. Thomson knew Stan's parents. He had run into Frank Sr. during his days as the town's works foreman, and the elder Koebel and his wife came out to the Thomson farm now and again to buy eggs. They were decent people. And Stan had always seemed dedicated and knew the ins and outs of the PUC. Maybe there was another explanation for what had happened. It made no sense to go around pointing fingers until all the facts were in. No. A quiet backroom chat, Thomson decided, was what was called for. No going off half-cocked. Maybe that was McQuigge's style. It wasn't his.

"Why did the public utilities commission tell the health unit the water was okay?" a reporter asked at an afternoon news conference.

"I can't honestly answer that question," Thomson responded.

When the PUC heard there was a problem, he continued, they started to flush the system and continued flushing diligently. It was only days later, he said, that E. coli was confirmed to be in the water. A half-hour later, in another TV grilling, the interviewer asked if the public had been notified as quickly as it should have been. That's a matter of opinion, Thomson replied. The Ministry of the Environment had only issued the boil-water advisory as a precaution, he said, getting his facts mixed up. During yet another TV interview at 6 P.M., he was asked whether enough had been done when people first started to show symptoms of illness. And again, he defended Stan Koebel and the public utilities commission. The PUC had acted very reliably, he said. After all, the manager had upped chlorine levels and begun flushing on Friday even though he didn't know anything was wrong.

McQuigge fumed. While Thomson had praised the health unit for acting appropriately during one of the interviews, he had said nothing about the adverse water samples, nothing about the defective chlorination, nothing about what Stan knew and didn't tell. Nothing! Throughout the afternoon, McQuigge voiced his concerns to his staff: it wasn't even close to being a matter of opinion about whether the public was notified as quickly as possible. Thomson's silence and prevarication amounted to letting the health unit's credibility hang out there in the wind. No. If the bloody diarrhea was going to hit the fan because of some dope at the public utilities commission and a wishy-washy mayor, none of the spatters was going to sully McQuigge. Besides, who would take the unit's urgent advice seriously if it were being tarred with the same dirty brush as those incompetents? He was still stewing as he drove home that evening, when a plan formed in his mind. People had to know why it had taken him two long days to issue the boil-water advisory. Telling the world what he knew carried the risk of upsetting the mayor, Stan Koebel, and perhaps others, thereby getting in the way of dealing with the crisis. If ever there was a time to be working together, this was it. But protecting his reputation had to take precedence. The time had come to set the record straight.

Wednesday, May 24
9:30 P.M.

"I'm going on the air first thing in the morning to tell all the media that this tragedy could have been prevented," McQuigge told the startled mayor by phone.

"Can't you wait, at least until after I've talked to council? We're meeting at 8 A.M., you know."

"No, I can't wait," McQuigge replied. "The public needs to know that this could have been prevented."

Thomson reluctantly acquiesced. McQuigge called Patterson.

"I'm going to be on *Canada AM* at seven in the morning," McQuigge told him. "I'm going to tell them everything we know."

Patterson set his alarm clock. This was one broadcast he wasn't going to miss. Five hours had passed since seventy-five-year-old

Vera Coe had died in the Walkerton hospital. She'd undergone a radical mastectomy for breast cancer nine days earlier and appeared to be recovering. She had developed symptoms of E. coli poisoning on the day the health unit put out the boil-water advisory.

Thursday, May 25
5:30 A.M.

Murray McQuigge sat down at his office computer and typed up the statement he had brooded over most of the night. The first glow of the new day was on the horizon when he headed down to the CTV satellite truck parked outside the front of the building. The TV crew was already waiting to do the interview that was scheduled to air live on the national show, *Canada AM*. McQuigge told them he wanted to make a statement and they passed that on to the studio in Toronto. Shortly after 7 A.M., interviewer Wei Chen's voice sounded in his earpiece.

"Have you ever seen anything like this?" she was asking.

"No. We've never seen anything like this."

"What's happened here? Why has this happened?"

"Well, I'm about to make a statement and it's a statement we'd prefer not to make."

On the street that parallels the Sydenham River just metres from where McQuigge stood, a truck went by. Chen gave him the go-ahead.

"Yesterday, there were questions of the chief medical officer of health of Ontario and myself about whether we acted with all possible speed to warn the citizens of Walkerton that their water might be contaminated," McQuigge began reading.

He recounted the events leading up to the boil-water advisory, including the calls his people had made to the PUC, although he didn't mention Stan Koebel by name. Several times, he emphasized that the PUC had assured the health unit the water was "safe and secure." The PUC had received a fax the previous

Thursday showing that the water was contaminated but had failed to notify anyone.

"On Sunday," he continued, "our investigation pointed to the water supply and we no longer believed what we were being told by the Walkerton PUC and we issued a boiling-water drinking advisory to the town of Walkerton and phoned the mayor of Walkerton to inform him.

"We told these findings to the Walkerton town council at a meeting that we called for at 2:00 P.M. on Tuesday."

Chen, who had been listening patiently to this point, could hardly believe her ears. Nothing in his tone had prepared her for what he had just said.

"Dr. McQuigge, Dr. McQuigge . . ." she interrupted.

"Yes?"

"Could I just get you to stop a moment?" Chen asked, her face incredulous.

"These public officials knew for some time that the water was contaminated and if they had informed the public, these deaths . . . ?"

"That's correct," McQuigge interjected.

"These people who are sick, this could have been prevented?" Chen managed to complete her sentence.

"These deaths could have been prevented," McQuigge agreed.

Chen looked past the camera, as if pleading with someone to rescue her.

"What is the explanation that they've given to you when you've confronted them?"

"I wish I knew," McQuigge went on. "There is no explanation for this, when we talked to them."

Chen looked stunned. She exhaled loudly.

"I can't believe that this negligence could happen," she said. She appeared to be genuinely angry.

Patterson grimaced as he watched. A cauldron of emotions churned within him and he fought back tears. It was all out now. He headed to Owen Sound. At the office, he and McQuigge embraced and cried. In the early-morning quiet, they shored up each other's spirits as they talked. The two men felt very alone in a world they thought had let them down badly.

"Folks, we needed to go public with this, and hopefully it will take the heat off the staff," McQuigge told the morning outbreak meeting.

But his defence of the health unit's credibility had poured gasoline on a brushfire. The crush of media intensified. The tragedy befalling Walkerton had entered an entirely new plane: it had been *preventable*, the deaths had been *preventable*. A stunned town, already reeling from the plague upon them, felt sick to the very soul. The world beyond, which had been watching with a mixture of grim bemusement and dismay, was horror-struck. *Preventable?* This was no accident? Walkerton, the obscure little town in the verdant Saugeen river valley, was suddenly infamous.

14

Shattered Trust

Thursday, May 24
7:45 A.M.

PUBLIC UTILITIES CHAIRMAN Jim Kieffer walked the few blocks from his tuxedo rental business to the council chambers after a telephone call saying the mayor wanted to see him and Stan Koebel.

"Where's Stan?" Dave Thomson asked.

"I just walked over," Kieffer responded. "I thought he'd be here."

"Look, I want to get the meeting going," Thomson said. "I've got other commitments. Would you please go and get him?"

Thomson handed his car keys to Kieffer.

"I guess he's working with some people trying to set up some more flushing. They were going to start the second flush of all the pipes and start working on the standpipes."

"Well, I want him down here and I want him down here now."

"What have you got in mind, anyway?" Kieffer asked.

"Suspend him without pay," Thomson responded.

Kieffer was surprised. The previous evening at Your Place, the restaurant attached to Rob's Sports Bar and Roadhouse next door to the municipal offices, Thomson hadn't mentioned that possibility.

"I don't think that's a good idea," Kieffer said.

"Why not?"

"Stan and Frank are the only two that really have any kind of understanding of the water system. If we suspend Stan, we might lose Frank as well. No one knows the system like they do. Besides, there's still the hydro to run."

"Well, go get him and we'll see."

Kieffer drove up to the PUC office, where he ran into Janice Hallahan. He asked her to call Stan's wife to see if she'd come down to the office.

"Is everything fine?" Hallahan asked, her face betraying what she already knew.

"It doesn't look good," Kieffer replied.

When he returned with Stan to the municipal building, Thomson called them into his office.

"Do you know where the problems were, what happened?" Thomson asked Stan, who looked even more haggard, despondent, and frightened than he had previously.

Once again, Stan repeated what had already been revealed at the meeting with McQuigge two days earlier, and at the council meeting the day before. Thomson was having trouble hiding his disappointment. As manager of the PUC, he felt Stan had owed it to him to say, "Yeah, the tests were bad and I knew we had a problem."

Still, Kieffer's advice appeared to have softened Thomson. He suggested Stan and Frank stay on and run the hydro side while the provincial Ontario Clean Water Agency would be asked to take over the water. Stan shook his head but said nothing. It was all over.

As soon as they had left, Thomson convened yet another special council meeting. For days he had given Stan the benefit of the doubt. As mayor, he had sat on his hands after McQuigge called him about the boil-water advisory on the Sunday. He had done nothing even after Stan told him the same day he was working on the system. He had then deflected, defended, waited. He had refused to believe that the man he had trusted had misled him. Suddenly, he could deny no more: Murray McQuigge's allegations about Stan were true. And the mayor realized that he, too, had been lying to the public. Thomson burst into tears. When he composed himself, council passed a resolution retaining the services of the Ontario Clean Water Agency for six months, a motion quickly rescinded when a lawyer noted only the PUC had that authority.

By the time Stan and Kieffer returned to the PUC office, Carole had arrived. Hallahan knew the media would be looking for Stan and suggested it was probably best to get him to a secure location. Stan and Carole talked it over briefly before deciding to head out of town to a friend's place for at least a couple of days. Stan gave Hallahan a telephone number where he could be reached and left. Minutes later, investigators from the Environment Ministry entered the PUC office, walked past the large poster in the small lobby that read Brockton Water Tastes Great!, and asked to see Stan.

"He's just left the building," Hallahan told them.

So they took Kieffer into Koebel's now abandoned office, closed the door, and began interrogating the bewildered part-time commissioner who had been acclaimed to his position four times.

Had an earthquake or tornado struck Walkerton, the damage would have been obvious. But the sunny streets bore no witness to the devastation being wreaked by an invisible killer that made its way through pipes hidden underground and in the walls of homes. "It looks the same, so how can it be bad?" one child asked of the tap water. It was a question everyone wanted answered. Still, except for the invasion of reporters, cameras, and satellite trucks, the town appeared eerily normal. Nothing alerted a casual observer to the pain and confusion, the grief and illness, or the terror that swept from house to house, fanned by screaming newspaper headlines and TV reports. Except, of course, for the sickening, gut-wrenching sound of the helicopters like some throbbing cosmic migraine. Every flight added to the feeling of dread. Who's next? Who's going to die? In the hospital about one hundred walking wounded waited in various states of pallid misery. As yet another helicopter took off, a nurse leaned against a corridor wall and slowly slumped to the floor in utter despair. Beneath the veneer of normalcy, daily life had been turned upside down. In homes around the town, hundreds and hundreds of people were coping with the ugly symptoms of E. coli. Frantic parents agonized over sick children, children over their sick parents. Almost everyone was either ill or knew someone who was. Grieving families prepared funerals. Day cares and schools were shut down, restaurants closed. Around town, signs sprang up on the roadsides. E. coli. Please Go Away or Pray for the Children of Walkerton. Store clerks donned gloves, bars served drinks in disposable plastic mugs. The smell of bleach began to permeate everything. At the popular Tim Hortons across the road from the stone house built by Joseph Walker, a large trailer with its own water supply sat in the parking lot to serve customers their daily fix of coffee and doughnuts. In the fresh morning air, reporters and photographers leaned against their cars drinking steaming coffee. They swapped stories about motels in which they couldn't shower before beginning yet another frantic, confusing round of news conferences and hospital visits and calls to head office. McQuigge's pronouncements had lent a new urgency to the story.

CBC Radio reporter Dave Seglins had been doing live reports via his Toronto newsroom when he heard McQuigge's comments. He was aghast. For several days, the doctor had been the voice of authority, the narrator, if you will, as the tragedy unfolded. But now a demon had suddenly emerged from the chaos in the form of Stan Koebel. On the spur of the moment, Seglins drove over to the PUC office, where he saw a man getting into a car. He walked over with his tape recorder.

"Hi," he said. "Sorry to bother you. But can you tell me who's in charge of the water?"

"I am," came the soft reply.

Until that moment, Seglins had had no idea he was looking at Stan Koebel, who appeared dolefully resigned to the questions that would follow. Seglins thrust his microphone in Stan's face.

"Did you know there was a problem with the water last Thursday?" he asked.

"I'm sorry, I can't say," came the dazed, seemingly robotic response. "Dave Thomson will explain everything later."

Seglins pressed him further.

"I'm sorry, I just can't say," he said before driving off into self-imposed exile. It was the first and last public comments Stan would make for months.

In London, a worried Doug Matsell, the hospital's chief pediatric kidney specialist, spoke to reporters:

"There are children in intensive care who are not getting better; they are getting worse," he said. "I cannot say there won't be more deaths. In fact, I worry that there will be more deaths."

Thursday, May 24
11:45 A.M.

Word of Murray McQuigge's pronouncements spread rapidly through town. Residents reeled from the notion that the catastrophe could have been, should have been, prevented. Several of them crashed a news conference, where Dave Thomson and Jim Kieffer were trying desperately to explain themselves. Terry Flynn, the town's newly hired media spokesman, had prepared a statement, which the nervous mayor read to the assembled reporters. Nothing in his world could ever have prepared him for this.

"At 10:00 P.M. last night, I received a telephone call from Dr. McQuigge, who informed me that he was going to release a statement to the media this morning on the sequence of events over the last week. Dr. McQuigge advised me that it was his opinion that the information that we were receiving from the public utilities commission may not be factual.

"As such, I requested a meeting this morning with the chair of the PUC, Mr. Jim Kieffer, and the general manager, Mr. Stan Koebel, to clarify the facts as we know them. I asked Mr. Koebel if in fact the PUC had had the results of testing for E. coli on May 18, 2000. He told me that he was aware that the PUC did receive analytical data from their lab on Thursday."

"If Mr. Koebel had the faxed lab results, why didn't he act sooner?" a reporter asked.

"Mr. Koebel said he did have the lab report on Thursday, May 18, but he did not believe it was as serious as it came to be," Thomson replied.

Thomson's right arm was shaking. He jammed his hand into his pants pocket in an effort to hide the tremor as reporters and residents went on the offensive.

"Why wasn't this information brought to the public right away?" shouted Phil Englishman, a part-time pilot and resident of the town.

"I did not ask that question," Kieffer said as he twisted and crumpled a piece of paper he was holding. "We were too busy trying to get the system flushed and chlorination into it. There were just too many things we were trying to track down."

"Is it true they didn't know the potential danger of E. coli?" asked another reporter as Kieffer sipped on bottled water and Thomson looked uncomfortable.

"At the particular time, yes," Kieffer stammered. Terry Flynn stealthily reached over and extracted the sheet of paper from his fiddling hand.

"Somebody is going to pay," one resident exploded. "These people are being paid. They should be fired."

"These guys are responsible for these people's deaths, as far as I'm concerned," came another angry voice.

Within hours, provincial police would begin swarming the town, adding to the confusion.

15

Welcome to Little Walkerton

Thursday, May 24
I P.M.

JANICE SMITH had just gotten home with five-year-old Tamara after yet another visit to the Walkerton hospital when the phone rang.

"Get her up here right now," a nurse told her. "She's going to London."

Like so many others, Janice hadn't thought too much of it when Tamara came down first with stomach cramps and then with diarrhea. And like so many others, she'd been to the Walkerton hospital several times, only to be sent home again each time. Tamara could barely get off the couch. Her brown, wavy hair was bedraggled, her normally bright green-brown eyes dull. By the time a week had gone by, the already compact little girl had lost enough weight for the loss to be noticeable. Her yellow pallor gave her the look of a jaundiced baby. Her lips were puffy and cracking, her thirst constant.

The nurses rushed the youngster into the ER and immediately hooked her up to an IV. Her dad, Brad Smith, took one look at her and went to pieces.

"I can't take it any more," he cried.

Hospital staff gave him a tranquilizer. They planned at first to transfer Tamara to London by ambulance but decided instead to send her by helicopter. Now it was Tamara's turn to be terrified. One of the flight paramedics gave her a teddy bear, with cuddly white fur, sympathetic brown eyes, and a blue scarf around its neck embossed with the word "Pioneer." As they wheeled her from the ER, she suddenly realized her bear was missing.

"Where's my teddy? Where's my teddy?"

Brad ran back inside to fetch it. The reporters and photographers waited.

"Are we going to cover her up?" the paramedic asked.

Brad nodded and they pulled the sheet over her head. As they wheeled her toward the awaiting helicopter, Canadian Press photographer Kevin Frayer began taking pictures from a distance. At that moment, a gust of wind blew the sheet off her face. Click. Across Canada and abroad, people picking up a newspaper the next morning saw little Tamara's face peeking out from a shroud of white sheets, her furrowed brow, half-closed eyes, and slightly open mouth exposing a mix of plaintive dread and exhaustion. Next to her head, the white bear lay on its back staring stoically into space, its fluffy arms outstretched as if to say, "Hold me." If there had been any misunderstanding as to depth of the trauma befalling the once sleepy town, that image dispelled it.

On a downtown sidewalk, an old man paused to gaze upward as the all-too-familiar noise filled the air.

"Oh sweet Jesus," he said aloud to no one in particular. "Not another one of our kids."

As Jamie and Cathy McDonald watched, increasingly exhausted Walkerton hospital staff prepared five-year-old Ian for an emergency ambulance run to London. He'd been admitted some thirty-six hours earlier when he began throwing up blood and

Jamie had told the nurse, "I can't do anything else for him. I'm losing him." Dark circles had formed around his eyes. His cheeks were hollowed. But it was only after Cathy noticed blood in his urine that the situation was deemed critical. A provincial police car acted as the ambulance escort. From the passenger seat, Cathy activated the cruiser siren, which burned out during the long drive to London.

So began their vigil. They noted every movement on their child's chart; platelets, hemoglobin, red and white blood cell counts rose and fell. It felt as if they'd been thrust onto some nightmarish roller coaster and all they could do was ride it out. Outside the ward someone had hung a sign: Welcome to Little Walkerton. Distraught relatives swapped stories and words of comfort. Some told how local motels had turned them away, as if they all were carriers of a plague. But it was the anxiety felt by dozens of worried parents that spread like contagion as their kids suddenly needed transfusions or got shipped down to dialysis. With every needle, tiny arms turned an uglier black and blue, while moms or dads clad in yellow hospital gowns helped hold them down.

"No more needles, no more," a child would plead, struggling uselessly against the inevitable.

A week after Tamara Smith had made her flight to London, she was deemed well enough to leave hospital, though she was so weak she could barely stand. She was disappointed to find out she'd be going by car. She wanted to go by helicopter.

For Jamie and Cathy McDonald, the thimble full of urine that Ian produced sent waves of joy through them. Until Jamie's mom, who'd been looking after Kylie and Alex, called from Owen Sound.

"Now don't worry," she said, "but Kylie has just tested positive for E. coli."

Jamie broke the news to Cathy, got into his car and headed to Owen Sound, while Cathy stayed behind to look after Ian. Within hours, the boy took a turn for the worse. The doctors had always warned he might need dialysis but said they'd give plenty of notice.

That evening, the doctor told Cathy it had become necessary. "When are you going to do it?" she asked.

"Immediately."

She ran to the phone to let Jamie know. Jamie had planned to stay the night with his parents so he could take Kylie to the Owen Sound hospital the following day for more tests. The couple agreed to stick to that plan. It was about 1:30 A.M. and Jamie had just drifted off to sleep when the ringing phone jolted him into instant consciousness. The anxiety-ridden voice of his wife sounded surreal.

"It's time to come down," she said.

Ian was dying. The doctor had inserted the dialysis catheter, but all he was getting was blood. A surgeon opened Ian up and found a hole in an artery, and was able to staunch the flow. He stitched the hole closed and gave the child a transfusion and blood products. Ian was still in desperate need of dialysis, but the method of pumping fluid into the abdomen wouldn't work because it simply poured back out of the surgical incision. So they put him on adult dialysis, itself risky for children, with a catheter inserted into a major blood vessel in his groin. Jamie arrived at about 3 A.M., courtesy of a colleague from the police detachment in Walkerton who drove him down in a cruiser. At the darkest of the hours before dawn, a doctor who had come up from Windsor to help in the E. coli treatment effort and who had himself been working non-stop for days walked over to the anguished parents. He was carrying coffee and doughnuts for them.

The new day had barely arrived when word came from Owen Sound: three-year-old Kylie had been admitted to hospital with failing kidneys. Dr. Kristen Hallett, who had sparked the search for the cause of the E. coli epidemic, consulted with her counterpart in the London hospital, which was fast reaching its limit to care for new patients. They discussed sending Kylie to Hamilton or Toronto but decided on London so the McDonald family could be together. With Ian in critical care, a pale and weakened Kylie was put upstairs in a ward for observation while Cathy helped hold her down so they could draw blood. In Owen Sound, two-year-old Alex felt completely abandoned. His grandparents agreed to drive him down to London so the family could be reunited. While one parent stayed with him at a motel, the other would run between floors, checking on their two sick children. Then Alex developed diarrhea as well, and Cathy and Jamie braced for a new round of fresh hell. It was a false alarm, likely caused by stress. Alex, possibly the most vulnerable of the three children, never did get E. coli poisoning. Because of recurring ear infections, he'd been on a maintenance dose of antibiotics, which likely saved him from contracting the gruesome illness. A night later, Ian began to pee and when his mom saw him eating some ice out of a cup, she knew the war had been won. Kylie, the most robust of the siblings, mended quickly without much further intervention. Two weeks after their nightmare began, the family was finally able to go back to a home they would soon leave again.

PART THREE

MURKY WATERS

16

Pride and Protest

LIKE MOST small communities in Canada, Walkerton has no door-to-door mail delivery. Instead, heading down to the post office is a peaceful ritual of daily life, a chance to greet friends and neighbours, catch up on the latest gossip, discuss the weather, pick up the mail. Now there was no place to park. Media vehicles and satellite trucks filled every available space as reporters milled about the building's entrance. Residents found themselves having to run a gauntlet of cameras and nosy big-city media types. Questions, questions, questions. Do you know anyone who's sick? Do you know anyone who has died? Who do you blame? What do you think of Stan Koebel? But the interlopers could never understand the conflicted emotions raised by every question about friends, neighbours, and family. How could these outsiders fathom the shock, the confusion, the grief and fear? The reporters, most of whom had never heard of Walkerton before being thrown into the assignment, would soon vanish like the snow on a warm April day, but *they* had to live here. Their presence was intrusive and ugly, their interest seemed almost prurient. They turned the funeral for Lenore Al into a circus befitting a rock star, instead of the sad farewell to a retired librarian whose widower was overcome by grief. That some of the local kids followed the cortege on their bicycles was wholly understandable. But vehicles emblazoned with media call letters? The only reporters and photographers they knew, often the same person, showed up at flower shows and minor-league hockey games and ribbon-cuttings and fundraising walkathons. How could these strangers possibly understand what they were going through? And so townsfolk developed a strategy: they marched into the post office with gaze averted. Eye contact or a smile would invariably be construed as an invitation to an interview. Reporters were perplexed. The small-town coldness, the hostility, made no sense. How could these people, upset as they must be, fail to understand their interest? It fell to those among the townspeople who were angry enough or who enjoyed the attention to satisfy the media's curiosity. Most Walkertonians felt sickened by what they read and saw.

Friday, May 26
1:30 P.M.

Far from the crowd gathered outside the post office and adjoining municipal building, a private plane carrying Ontario Premier Mike Harris cruised the almost cloudless, pale blue sky toward the airport outside Hanover. The wind was light, a perfect spring day for flying. From his window, the premier could see a checkerboard of fields with their intricate ploughing patterns offset by swaths of green meadows and patches of bush. In the airport building, Conservative legislature member Bill Murdoch munched on a hamburger. The tarmac was empty, save for a news helicopter off to one side. To the left of the airport building, a dark green Honda minivan, the favoured vehicle for moving the premier around, waited outside the iron gate that opened directly onto the tarmac. The plane landed, taxied to the middle of the tarmac, and came to a stop as the engines died. A man with mirrored sunglasses drove the minivan to within about fifteen metres of the plane. A reporter followed. A few minutes later, the door opened. The stairs lowered and Hillary Stauth, Harris's bubbly twenty-something junior communications assistant, emerged into the sunshine. She looked confused, as if she'd been expecting a crowd. It seemed so quiet.

"I hear CNN's here," she said, as if she couldn't quite believe it.

A few minutes later, Harris emerged at the top of the stairs. Dressed in a dark blue sports jacket and light blue open-necked shirt, he looked decidedly unhappy. He moved quickly down the stairs, strode to the minivan without a sideways glance, and got in. The van disappeared through the gate for the ten-minute run to Walkerton.

The van took him to the back of the municipal building. Harris slipped inside and met privately with Mayor Dave Thomson. Although he had little grasp of the staggering magnitude of the situation, Thomson told Harris that the municipality was facing something it couldn't handle alone and the premier promised to do what he could. Outside, in the now blazing sun, an impatient media crowd waited. Harris's arrival had been set for about 1 P.M., but he was running close to an hour late. Behind and to the right of a row of TV cameras and reporters, a clutch of about forty residents, adults and children, had gathered. Across the road lined with cars, news vehicles, and satellite trucks, a few pre-teen boys took pictures. Walkerton had never seen anything like this. Just behind one of the TV cameras, a boy put down the puppy he'd been carrying.

"Has your dog been sick as well?" one reporter asked.

"Yeah, he's been a little sick," the kid replied gravely.

Hillary Stauth emerged from the municipal office through the glass door to the right of the post office. The premier would be out in a few minutes, would make a statement, and then take questions. To keep it orderly, she said, she would give the signal to each reporter. It was clear this was going to be a tightly controlled, conventional news conference. Someone to one side asked if the premier would take questions from the public. Stauth made a note, said something to the man, and disappeared inside.

Moments later, Harris came through the glass door and strode the few steps over to the brown podium set up on the concrete boulevard. Bill Murdoch and rookie Environment Minister Dan Newman stood awkwardly against the red-brick wall of the municipal office. His mouth turned down, his face grim, his brow furrowed, Harris placed a piece of paper on the podium, waited a few seconds for the TV cameras to get rolling, and began reading:

"I come to this community under very tragic circumstances," he read. "I come today not only as premier, but I come as a father, I come as a son, I come as a fellow citizen who has been touched by the events of this week. I come on behalf of an entire province and indeed an entire country that has been moved and deeply saddened and brought together by what is happening here."

Mike Harris, it is fair to say, had never been celebrated for his oratorical skills. During question period or in dealing with the usual media crowd at the legislature, he had shown himself highly capable of spontaneous flashes of wit and charged partisan rhetoric. That was a game he'd mastered. However, a natural stump speaker he wasn't. Under the right circumstances and at his best, the premier could deliver a speech that engaged an audience even if it didn't quite captivate them. At his worst, his dull monotone and stiff, wooden style gave the impression that he didn't quite believe or feel the words coming out of his own mouth.

"For today, Walkerton is Ontario and Walkerton is Canada," he continued as the silent crowd listened intently.

"All of us, all Canadians, are united with the families of Walkerton. United in grief, we are united in prayer, we are united in heart, and we are united in mind. We are united in the determination to stand by one another until this situation passes.

"I have directed that all necessary resources of the Ontario government be made available to help the citizens of this community weather this storm. I pledge that we will do what it takes to get to the bottom of this tragedy. The people of Walkerton demand answers. People of Ontario demand answers. And I demand answers. But that is an issue for tomorrow.

"Today, our thoughts rest with the families of this community, with everyone that is struggling to cope with these tragic events, and standing beside them I believe is the first priority, and that is the first priority reason that I am here."

On paper, the words appeared to have exactly the right sound, the right balance of empathy and concern. But as he spoke them in the hot sun, glancing up only to look at the cameras in his practised way, they appeared to lose all flavour, all real sentiment, all resonance. His flat, lowered voice betrayed little, if any, emotion. It felt too carefully prepared, overcooked, insipid. The crowd remained quiet.

"I'll take questions," he said quickly.

CBC reporter Raj Ahluwalia immediately jumped in. He asked about the changes the Conservative government had made after coming to office in 1995. Could the Tories' decision to privatize water-testing have contributed to the crisis? Harris fiddled with the front of his jacket.

"Well, I am told there are no changes," Harris began.

Harris went on to say that if any government policies or procedures had played a role, it wasn't his regime that had implemented them. Look to the New Democrats, who had formed the government before him, he said. The tragedy had become a partisan political football.

Almost immediately upon coming to power in June 1995, the Harris government had taken the axe to the Environment Ministry, slashing its budget and staff as it tackled the province's $10-billion annual deficit with single-minded purpose. Warnings from scientists, health professionals, and even the most senior bureaucrats about the debilitating and demoralizing effects of the cuts went unheeded. While the NDP had governed during one of the deepest recessions since the Great Depression and had made some staff cuts, it was under the Harris government that, for the first time, hundreds of ministry employees were forced out the door. Helping business and industry topped a Conservative agenda designed to balance the province's books and cut taxes. Environmental rules and regulations, such as one requested by the minister of health himself to clarify the reporting of bad water, were rejected as red tape that simply got in the way of much needed job-creation. From on high, the word came down that strenuous enforcement of environmental rules was not wanted. "Partnerships," "stakeholders," and "voluntary compliance" became the new buzzwords. The number of prosecutions, convictions, and fines levied against polluters fell sharply. The number of inspections of waterworks declined. The ministry's traditional role as watchdog over the province's ecological integrity and its water quality had been dangerously undermined. Harris said nothing about any of that.

If Mike Harris wasn't known for his rousing speeches, he'd also never been known for his warmth or exuberance. He could be amiable enough, but he seldom appeared to be at ease in a crowd. He did not indulge in phony baby-kissing. Perhaps that was part of his appeal. He seemed to be a genuine, down-to-earth fellow who had little use for touchy-feely antics in order to win votes. But to a town desperately in need of a warm, steadying hand and a show of solidarity and leadership, Harris seemed indifferent.

The hardline policies and confrontational approach that marked the Conservatives' years in office, especially those of their first term, had made Harris a target for protests both big and small. He'd been dogged at every stop during his re-election campaign in the spring of 1999 by small, vocal groups of dissenters. Through it all, Harris remained dismissive, even contemptuous. He portrayed every voice of opposition as coming from a "special interest group" to which he would never listen. Labour unions, teachers, civil servants, mothers on welfare had all felt the sting. His supporters, and they were many across the province, including Walkerton, liked his strength of conviction, his willingness to forge ahead with what he believed. But Harris seemed to view the townsfolk gathered outside their post office as just another special interest group. He offered no personal words of encouragement, gave no sign he really cared, no indication that he had come for any other reason than to bolster his own political interest. He gave no hint that he understood the calamity that had visited this rural town. Instead of applying balm to soothe their wounds, he had rubbed in partisan salt. Without so much as a glance at the people who looked to him as their leader and friend, Ontario Premier Mike Harris turned away and disappeared into the municipal offices.

When he had first approached the microphone, Harris had stared briefly at a crudely crafted protest sign directly in front of him, the only one in evidence: We Demand Answers. No More Cutbacks. The sign seemed to confirm that the gaggle of people clustered around the protester were just another anti-Tory special interest group. In fact, had Harris looked to see who was holding the sign, he'd have noticed a slightly weathered man in his mid-fifties, a man who had never demonstrated before, a man who had given the premier and his Conservative party his vote in both of the previous provincial elections, the second one barely ten months earlier.

Dieter Weiss owned the old foundry property on the edge of town, directly across from Lobie's Park. The foundry, one of the first manufacturing plants in the province, dated back to Joseph Walker's days. Horse ploughs and the like had been made there in a plant that drew its power through a water wheel on the Saugeen River before the Walkerton Electric & Power Company provided electricity. The plant closed in the late 1980s, and Weiss bought the site with the retirement aim of turning it into a tourist-type canoeing and fishing recreation area. The river was thick with salmon and trout, but as the years went by, the fish slowly disappeared.

The huge Friday-night rainstorm had swamped the site. The overflowing Saugeen drowned the foundry in forty centimetres of putrid water. The stench of manure sickened him. Despite being an old farm boy, Weiss had become increasingly disconcerted with what he considered to be Big Agriculture's maltreatment of the environment. Over the previous four or five summers, beaches along his favourite strip of Lake Huron had to be closed due to bacterial contamination, sparking finger-pointing between farmers and cottagers. He bridled at what he saw as the irresponsible spraying and spreading of vast quantities of manure and pesticides on fields because it would inevitably wash into nearby waterways, killing minnows, frogs, and other aquatic life. Although he complained to anyone who might listen, the powerful agricultural lobby had the ear of the politicians. No one had the guts to take them on, certainly not in a town like Walkerton that depends so heavily on its farm neighbours.

Weiss felt sure the poisonous water coursing through the town's taps had to be farm-related. But, he said to friends, no one would investigate. Even the mayor was a farmer. There would be a cover-up. There's nothing you can do, they said. The hell you can't, he replied. Though he had never taken part, images of the 1960s' civil rights and anti-Vietnam War demonstrations had left an indelible impression on him. People had marched and carried signs and, ultimately, someone had listened. Still, the idea of demonstrating terrified him. It was a front-page newspaper photograph that steeled his determination to act. Tucked into a stretcher next to her teddy bear, five-year-old Tamara Smith was about to be airlifted for treatment to London. Dieter Weiss pondered the photograph, and cried. Tamara could just as easily have been his granddaughter.

On hearing that the premier was coming to town that afternoon, Weiss headed to his workshop at the foundry and scrounged up the most quintessential of Canadian artifacts: an old canoe paddle. Next, he found a piece of plywood, and a sign was born. Now, the hard part: What's it to say? Harris is an asshole? No. He had no desire to offend the man he'd twice voted for. He had approved of many of Harris's policies: work-for-welfare, the downsizing of the bloated bureaucracy. But the cuts to the Environment Ministry bothered him, especially because big farmers appeared to have been given free rein to pollute the environment, his environment, his grandchildren's environment. And so he scrawled: We Demand Answers. No More Cutbacks. His friends were dismayed. You could be arrested, they said. You could be clubbed or pepper-sprayed, they said. You're going to get your ass kicked, you'll be tarred and feathered and run out of town, they said. Weiss considered. What he needed, he realized, was support. People power. So he sped over to Ron Leavoy's print shop on Durham and asked for a rush job on five hundred flyers advertising a protest for the following day. "Come to our meeting to preserve our clean water and air and stop the cutbacks," the flyers said.

"I don't know if we can get this done," Leavoy told him.

"It's your grandchildren that are affected," Weiss rejoined.

The flyers were printed. He plonked down the $50 and headed back to his shed, retrieved his newly minted sign, and began what surely must have been one of the loneliest and strangest protest marches the town had ever seen. Clutching the pile of flyers in one hand, the sign in the other, he made his way over the bridge across Durham and up the lower end of Yonge Street toward the post office. A reporter spotted him.

"You're a lone voice in the wilderness," she said. "Where are your supporters?"

"I don't expect any," he replied.

All he wanted, Weiss explained, was to talk to the premier, to ask him the environmental questions that were bothering him. Already he suspected that Stan Koebel was going to take the fall and it would then be business as usual. But no matter what the town's water manager had or hadn't done, he felt the problem ran far deeper. He was shocked when he turned the corner onto Scott Street and sighted the horde of media assembled in front of the post office. That he hadn't expected. The mayor, a flock of councillors in tow, passed him on their way to Newman's for lunch. They glared and refused to take a flyer from him. Almost no one would, except for a couple of reporters who feigned interest. No way they were going to be taken in by some half-crazed old geezer with a beef and a sign, not with a far bigger news story set to happen. A few motorists quietly gave him the thumb's up or timidly honked their horns as they drove by, but that was it for support. It didn't bother Weiss. To and fro he walked. To and fro. Then, perhaps fed up with having nothing better to do while he hurried up and waited for the main event, a reporter at last moseyed over.

"Why are you doing this? Isn't this a local problem?"

"It's all over Ontario," he replied. "Do you think all the E. coli in the province washed down our well?"

Weiss waxed on about the damage caused by the wanton spreading of manure and pesticides: the dead minnows and frogs, the closed beaches. And suddenly other reporters were lining up to talk to him as well. Harris's lateness offered more time for interviews. Each time, he passed on the simplest of messages:

"I have children and grandchildren. I don't want them to live in a garbage dump."

When Hillary Stauth emerged from behind the glass doors to survey the lie of the media land and say Harris would be out shortly, Weiss had already joined the small clutch of townsfolk standing to her left. He asked if the premier would take questions from the public. Stauth jotted the comment down, said she'd see what she could do before going back inside. Suddenly, a uniformed local police officer standing just behind him and to his left put his hand on the shoulder of the man with the sign and hissed:

"Dieter, you know what you did back there."

He turned his head toward the officer.

"What do you mean?"

"Jumping in front of the cameras. I don't want to see any more of that."

"I did not jump in front of the cameras. I was politely asked and I obliged."

A burly man pushed his way behind Weiss, and the lone protester, who was becoming increasingly nervous, knew it was an undercover officer appraising the threat. Weiss worried about being pepper-sprayed or dragged off to jail. The hot spring air felt charged. Minutes later, a hush fell on the crowd as Harris emerged and began his speech to the media. Weiss listened quietly, patiently. The reporters were almost done and he could wait no longer. "Mr. Harris, Mr. Harris," he called out, to no avail.

The uniformed police officer behind him tapped him yet again on the shoulder.

"Keep it down or else," he growled.

Dieter Weiss had never given up on democracy even though it had never seemed to work very well for him. He exercised his franchise zealously. He voted on the issues he cared about rather than for the personalities or parties. Each time, it felt as if his vote had been stolen from him. He had backed the federal Liberals under Pierre Elliott Trudeau, at least until he turned the country metric. He voted for the federal Conservatives when Brian Mulroney promised jobs, jobs, jobs, then watched in dismay as the jobs went to Mexico. When Jean Chrétien promised to scrap the federal sales tax introduced by the Mulroney Tories, he voted Liberal again but the GST remains a fact of Canadian life. Provincially, he had backed the Liberals under David Peterson when they promised to make beer available in corner stores. But they reneged on that pledge and so, in 1990, he voted for the New Democrats of Bob Rae because they promised cheap, publicly run car insurance. That, too, didn't happen. But he liked what Harris and his provincial Tories were saying in 1995, and so he voted for them, and again in 1999 because he felt Harris was a politician who knew how to get things done. Still, he wished the premier would get his people to research the effects of all those cuts to the Environment Ministry a little better and he wanted badly to ask Harris about that. Weiss wheeled to face the cop.

"We don't live in Communist Russia. We don't live in a dictatorship. I'm here to ask a question, now back off."

The officer began reaching for his truncheon, but a TV camera swung toward them and the club stayed put. By this time, Harris had vanished, leaving resident Veronica Davidson shrieking after him and taking the pressure off Weiss and his furiously pounding heart. He had received no answers. He hadn't even gotten to ask his question. He felt deeply offended and deeply disappointed. As reporters rushed off to file their stories, the crowd dispersed. When someone mentioned that Harris was going to the arena where donated bottled water was being passed out, Weiss jumped into his truck and followed after him. It was too late. Harris had dropped a few bucks into a collection jug and left town. Weiss dropped $20 of his own into the jug and went home. He put his sign away and spent the rest of the day waiting in dread for a knock at the door that would tell him he was off to jail. It didn't, of course, come. No one, if you discount the media and the Davidsons, who came with their ginger-haired offspring in tow, showed up the following day for the big protest that Weiss had tried to organize. Not even Weiss.

Veronica Davidson had also come down to the post office to hear what Premier Mike Harris had to say that Friday afternoon and she didn't like what she heard. When the premier abruptly disappeared through the glass door, the drama teacher exploded.

"Mr. Harris!" she shouted after him. "It's a shame you have to go off quickly and not hear those points of view of the people who live in Walkerton."

As cameramen, photographers, and reporters jostled to get closer, Davidson unloaded. For a moment, it was as if the entire town's anger was being channelled through this short, ginger-haired mother of two.

"We are a small town, we have dealt with death," Davidson said, her voice rising over the din, as if that would help her words reach the ears of the now vanished premier.

"We have seen the system obviously does not work," she said, hands flailing. "And now that you've seen the system doesn't work, are you going to put a system in place so this type of tragedy never has to happen again?"

She paused to spell her name for one of the reporters.

"It seemed like a lot of platitudes without substance. I waited patiently, with respect, to see what he would say, and when he did not say anything, then I felt it was necessary to speak up. I think he needs to address us personally. I don't think he can hide behind all kinds of protocol."

From their home on the hill, Davidson's bemused husband watched Harris and then his wife on TV. While her roots in the area go back a century, Bruce Davidson was a newcomer of fourteen years to Walkerton. Born of Jamaican parents in the Toronto suburb of Scarborough, Bruce had met Veronica during their university years in Guelph, Ontario. For a while, Bruce flirted with making a career in theatre, and worked behind the scenes as a technician at a small company in Toronto. But when Veronica went on to pursue a career in teaching, Bruce opted to qualify as a registered massage therapist. It was Jim Kieffer, now chairman of the public utilities commission, who processed Bruce's Ontario driver's licence, sold him a pair of pants, and rented them their first Walkerton home, a townhouse. This is the only place, Davidson liked to quip, where you can find an ear, nose, and goat specialist. Although his family had escaped illness because they had been out of town, four people on their stretch of street had been airlifted to city hospitals. He had watched the confusion, terror, and heartache unfold as the glare of the national and international media grew increasingly harsh. He had watched the news conferences with Mayor Dave Thomson and Jim Kieffer and got no answers. It seemed to him as if things were out of control, that no one in charge was taking charge. The town's two main grocery stores had ordered in skids of bottled water, but council had failed to act. Walkerton was fast on its way to becoming North America's leper colony, but all the Davidsons saw that Friday from their provincial government, from their premier, was political posturing and denial. Even worse, they felt as if Mike Harris had simply ignored them. But if Veronica's tirade was heard across Canada and beyond, it resounded most loudly in her own backyard, in a shell-shocked community that had yet to find a voice to ask the hard questions, to express the depths of its frustration. At the Davidsons' home, the phone began ringing as friends and acquaintances called to let her know she had expressed *them*. And in that heady rush, Bruce began pondering a way to ensure that the community would stay heard, whether or not the premier and his allies in far-away Toronto wanted to listen.

Out of a conversation with his old activist neighbour Chris Peabody, a teacher at Sacred Heart and a future town councillor, a plan began taking shape. Davidson sat down at his computer and wrote a letter to the premier demanding a judicial inquiry into the disaster. He quickly garnered fourteen signatures and headed down to the local print shop to get the letter photocopied. There, he got talking with owner Ron Leavoy, whom he hadn't met before. Leavoy, whose daughter had been thwacked on the head by an overzealous TV cameraman at the Harris news conference outside the post office, signed immediately and the letter was faxed to Premier Mike Harris and copied to other politicians.

Soon, the leaders of the Opposition would visit the Davidsons' home and impress on the sixteen or twenty people gathered there that they needed to get organized. So a steering committee was formed and Concerned Walkerton Citizens (CWC) was born. Ron Leavoy became chairman, Bruce Davidson was elected vice-chair, and Veronica named secretary. Todd Huntley, who had once wondered why a girl couldn't buy a slush at the Becker's, became treasurer. Leavoy printed flyers advertising their first public meeting and other volunteers papered the town with them. About two hundred people showed up at the old Hartley House in mid-June and most signed on as members. Within weeks, the group grew to a signed-up membership of more than five hundred, 10 per cent of the town's entire population. Still, some people hated what Bruce and his group were doing. "You don't speak for me," the father of one of the town's elected politicians chastised him. "Who the hell does he think he is?" was another comment heard around town.

"There are some people who believe that if we deny, we will go back to being Walkerton," Davidson told one reporter.

The CWC would not be denied. The politicians in Toronto were starting to listen and Bruce Davidson, whose biggest public speaking event had been as valedictorian at massage school grad-uation, became an articulate, persistent voice of Walkerton's residents, perhaps *the* voice. Slightly balding with curly hair, just five-foot-six-feet tall, he possessed the perfect turn of phrase, an intuitive understanding of what reporters needed, and first-hand knowledge of the town. Most importantly, he was willing to share what he knew, ask the questions few others in the community dared ask, and make himself available for a dizzying array of media interviews. Papers ranging from the *New York Times* and the *Manchester Guardian* to the weekly *Walkerton Herald-Times* talked to him. TV crews paraded through his home, sometimes lining up outside as they waited their turn. A CBC national TV crew spent three days doing "a day in the life of," following the family as they brushed their teeth with bottled water or drove the kids to a nearby town for a bath. Sociology students called asking if they could study the group as an example of an effective grassroots organization. Someone from the British Columbia government asked to use its resources. And through it all, Davidson marvelled at just how much attention he and the group continued to get.

17

Going Back Home

Only the most hardened miscreant, or blithering idiot, faces the prospect of criminal charges with any kind of equanimity. Stan Koebel was neither. As with most people, whose brushes with the law might comprise a parking-meter violation or speeding ticket, the prospect of being a hunted man was truly terrifying. For Stan, who two weeks earlier had been the respected manager of the Walkerton Public Utilities Commission, it was beyond terror. People were dead. God only knew how many more were ill or might die. How could this be? He'd flushed, and flushed and flushed. Hell, why hadn't anyone warned him? How on earth could he face those who had trusted him? How could he admit what he'd done, what he hadn't done? Dr. McQuigge had said the deaths were preventable. Did that make him a killer? A reckless monster? But look how hard he'd worked for so long. Look how well he'd done. Waves of anguish swept over him. Uncomprehending. How could this be? Who to talk to? Who to trust? What about Frank? With two heart attacks behind him, could Frank take the stress? Stan was inconsolable.

"I want him here today," Bill Trudell told Carole.

Trudell, a prominent criminal lawyer practising in Toronto, had defended some of society's worst offenders. People like Gary Foshay, the hitman who'd executed Hanna Buxbaum, a mother of six, on the side of a London-area highway at the behest of her whacked-out millionaire husband. Then there was James Ruston, a seventeen-year-old Petro-Canada gas-station attendant and a "kid worth saving," as Trudell put it. When Joseph Fritch, a corporate executive and father of four, tried to pay for his gas one night, Ruston pulled a garbage bag over his head while a buddy smashed his skull with a fire extinguisher and stole his wallet. Stan, of course, was different. This was a lost soul floundering in its own private hell. Trudell immediately arranged to get Stan to a psychiatrist. He also knew reporters, police, and ministry investigators all wanted to talk to his client.

"You have a right not to say anything. Don't talk to anybody, not even your brother," Trudell told him.

"Would you see Frank?" Stan asked.

Trudell agreed and Frank arrived the next day. He, too, was quiet and overwhelmed. Bill gave him the same brief advice he'd given Stan, had a psychiatrist talk to him, and referred him to fellow lawyer Mike Epstein.

It seemed self-evident to Trudell that Stan should not return to Walkerton and he told him so. Besides his client's state of mind, there was no telling who would be burned by the firestorm unleashed by McQuigge. But Trudell was also acutely aware that Stan appeared to have gone into hiding. The inference could only be that he had something to hide. Still, much as he might want to, Stan couldn't go back home, at least not until the time was right.

The right time was to come within days. Tuning into CBC Radio, Trudell heard an interview with the pastor at Walkerton's Trinity Lutheran Church, which Stan had joined after his divorce from Mary and remarriage to Carole.

"My congregation very strongly sends Stan their love, as do many, many people in the community," Pastor Beth Conroy was saying.

"Even those parents who have sick children in the hospital are saying, 'Tell Stan we understand that nothing is ever one person's fault and we're waiting to hear what has really happened.'"

Trudell knew it was time for Stan to go home. The psychiatrist agreed. Trudell called Conroy.

"He wants to come home, but he wants to see you," he said.

One of Walkerton's claims to fame as county town is its jail, where Stan's youngest brother Ken worked as a security guard. You pass it on the left as you go up Jackson Street a few blocks south of Durham Street. The structure has been there from the town's earliest days. In the 1860s, young John Hoag was sentenced to the gallows for killing a man in a drunken rage over a woman. Hoag was duly hanged behind the jail's imposing stone walls. The town doctor pronounced him dead and the body was placed in a coffin for burial in a plot outside town. A few weeks later, the judge who'd condemned him to death ran into a very much alive Hoag in the northern United States. Turns out, Hoag's desperate dad had prevailed upon the doctor to show sympathy to his wayward boy. In turn, the doctor had prevailed upon the hangman, who went along with a scheme to save the wretched youth. They fitted a harness and hook under his coat to which they attached the gallows rope. The death plunge wasn't. Out of sight of prying eyes, the live body was retrieved from the casket, which was filled with stones and buried. The episode was later memorialized in the syndicated newspaper series, *Ripley's Believe It or Not!* Walkerton was featured in *Ripley's* again on another occasion, when it recognized the town's uniqueness in having a jail with four churches on its four corners. Punishment and redemption located within a stone's throw of each other in a community whose solid religious underpinnings date back to Joseph Walker's times.

Beth Conroy was in effect the religious elder in Walkerton even though she only had five years in the town. The United Church minister had just retired, although his retirement tea had to be put off for months because of the crisis. The Presbyterian position was vacant, and the Pentecostal Church had yet to fill its vacancy. The Anglican part-time pastor lived outside town, while Father Paul Reilly, who headed the town's Roman Catholic Church, by far the largest, had been in place for only a year. The result was that Pastor Beth became the spiritual voice of the community throughout the crisis, a status reinforced by the fact that Stan belonged to her church. She had come to Walkerton to serve the 250-strong Lutheran congregation from the small southern Ontario community of Fisherville, where she'd seen another environmental disaster up close. The nearby town of Hagersville made international headlines in 1989 when a mammoth fire at a used tire dump burned uncontrollably for seventeen days, spewing choking black smoke and poison that smeared the community. The tire fire had hurt Hagersville badly, but its ugly blackness paled in significance to the hurt in Walkerton. Conroy found herself spending more and more time in the hospital, offering support, comfort, and a willing ear. Never had she experienced such intense suffering. It felt as if a Biblical plague had befallen the town, like some grotesque punishment for sins unimaginable. Now and again, as she listened to both the grief and anger, her eyes rolled back in their sockets, as if scanning some inner horizon in search of strength and wisdom to stay afloat as an emotional tidal wave threatened to swamp her.

Conroy knew the Koebels well. Both were regulars. Stan was always there whenever anything needed doing: washing the dishes or helping clean up the lawns after functions. She instantly agreed to Trudell's request that she see Stan. Trudell remained worried. He climbed into a car with the psychiatrist, while Stan and Carole took their own car. En route, Trudell called Dennis Player, Walkerton's acting chief of police, to ask advice. Player was immediately receptive.

"Where do you want to go? We'll help you," Player assured him.

Conroy met them outside town for a brief chat, and they all headed to the church, Trudell filled with trepidation at the reception they'd find. As they emerged from their cars, two passersby instantly recognized Stan, who was dressed in a checkered, open-necked, short-sleeve shirt, a lottery ticket protruding from his breast pocket.

"Hi, Stan, how are ya?" called the one.

"Hey, Stan, nice to see ya," the other said.

At that moment, Trudell knew he had nothing to worry about. And so did his client. It was time to face the media. Through his long career, Trudell had raised the sympathy game to a fine art, earning himself the nickname Weeping Willie in certain legal circles. But playing the sympathy card was dangerous. Like everyone else, he had little idea what had gone down or what might be uncovered. Still, as a defence lawyer, he had to remind the world that an accused remains innocent until proven guilty, that Stan deserved the benefit of the doubt. With the TV cameras rolling, photographers flashing, and reporters scribbling, Trudell read a statement he'd prepared earlier, a plea to give his client, who stood so forlornly at his side, some desperately needed breathing space.

"Mr. Koebel has come home to his community and wants to stay here. This is the community that he and his family love and which they have served for many years. He is a man who is suffering a great deal along with many others. He has been devastated with the loss of lives and suggestions that he or anyone is to blame.

"However, he is very grateful for the compassion and understanding which has been shown and he believes and trusts in the sense of fairness in this community and indeed in this country.

"This is a horrible tragedy that no one wanted, no one planned. On behalf of his family he asks that the members of the media respect their privacy and I, too, ask you to be compassionate and fair. Mr. Koebel is currently under a doctor's care. He is fine, but of course will be making no statement at this time."

Holding hands with his wife, Carole, and daughter, Stephanie, who flanked him, and with Pastor Beth keeping a respectful distance behind, Stan entered the church. At the quiet, private reunion, the family talked, hugged, and wept. It had been exactly five days since Stan had dropped out of sight.

Many in the media thought it more than passing strange that almost everyone seemed so willing to protect the man who appeared to have done them such an egregious wrong. But Stan was one of them, and his family was a mainstay of their community. They knew in their hearts that he'd never have intentionally caused them harm. And they didn't need outsiders to tell them how to react or to ask endless questions about anger and blame. They wanted answers, but instinctively they understood that no one man could possibly have borne responsibility for such an enormous calamity. The media might have wanted to see blood, but there would be none of that here. So Stan went back to his small bungalow at 902 Yonge Street, a kilometre or so up the road from the jail, to the refuge of the yard he'd tended so many times. Sure, there were a couple of crank calls and one person drove by the house and yelled, "You're a killer," but Stan was home, where he belonged. It wouldn't last. It couldn't last. It didn't.

18

A Town Under Siege

FROM ACROSS the country and abroad, hearts and wallets opened up for the rural town whose name everyone now seemed to know. Relief supplies poured in as people, small businesses, and large companies from near and far donated money, bottled water, bleach, toothbrushes, showerheads, food and food supplements, and other supplies. For its part, the provincial government announced an emergency relief package to cover out-of-pocket expenses for both individuals and businesses hit by the crisis. But despite the largesse and sympathy, and even as the urgency of caring for the sick and burying the dead eased, the town's shock and anger turned to depression. A blanket of despair began to settle over the besieged community. Out-of-town school teams cancelled games in Walkerton, or told the town's teams to stay away. Stories circulated about how a family from the town had been asked to leave a restaurant in Hanover, or how store clerks were afraid to handle money from Walkerton shoppers. Businesses struggled to stay afloat, if they were able to open at all. Employees were ill. Patrons stayed away. Who would

want to eat in a Walkerton restaurant, stay in a Walkerton motel?
People showed up at work, eyes red from the chlorine in the
shower water. Hands turned raw. Homes smelled of bleach.
Children began exhibiting symptoms of post-traumatic stress
disorder. Had they been sent away to live with a relative or friend
because they'd been bad? Where were their buddies? Offered a
chance to look inside a real helicopter, one little boy recoiled in
horror. That, he said, would mean being taken away, maybe to
die. Another child hid a bout of diarrhea from his parents. He
didn't want to end up being flown off to a big-city hospital as had
happened to a playmate down the street. Parents worried as they
kept kids away from taps and out of the lawn sprinkler that is
every child's right on a hot summer day. Each day, people filled
containers of water from a tanker or picked up donated bottles
of water from the arena and lugged them home or dragged them
up stairs. Mundane chores, washing vegetables, brushing teeth,
doing the dishes, giving the kids a bath, became a constant
reminder of the abnormal situation in which they lived. One
time, Lloyd Cartwright reached for the bottle of water next to
the basin to rinse his mouth. He accidentally grabbed the bleach
bottle next to it, a slip that left him with nasty burns to his mouth
and lips. His wife Marie's bridge team decided to skip the
regional tournament. They just didn't feel welcome. The arena,
packed almost to the rafters with donated bottled water, cancelled
the normal events that provide the fun and games that help bind
a community. Baseball diamonds, usually filled with the friendly
rivalry of area teams playing ball, were empty. One night, a bunch
of youngsters at a typically teenage loose end opened the tap on
the giant water tanker and left it gushing. Residents coming to
fill their bottles the next day were dismayed to find it empty. The
Concerned Walkerton Citizens intervened. A new tanker would
come and this time there would be security. But the plan was
scrapped when someone decided that tanker water was vulnerable to contamination anyway. Instead, only bottled water, this
time courtesy of the provincial government, would be made available. Strangers intruded into every home, leaving red tags on
water mains and concentrated chlorine solutions in every pipe

and every tap as the tedious, painstaking task of cleaning the
system got underway. Streets were dug up as underground mains
were located and replaced. The remediation bill began mounting into the millions of dollars. Who would pay? How long would
it last? What would happen to the children who had been so
deathly ill? When, in God's name, would it just be over? No one
could say. Mayor Dave Thomson retreated behind his communications firm and his lawyer, Rod McLeod. Town hall meetings
designed to provide information left townsfolk angry, frustrated,
and wholly unenlightened. They felt cut off from their civic
leaders, mistrustful of their provincial politicians, and denied
straight answers. Prime Minister Jean Chrétien had sent a
message of sympathy, but no one from the federal government
dared enter the political swamp that Walkerton was becoming.
Still, to the casual eye, the town stood as it always had. There had
been no earthquake. No devastating fire. No tornado. It all
looked so normal. Why then was everyone so gloomy?

For Rita Halpin, it felt like the war again, when the menfolk in
her family disappeared overseas to fight, many never to return.
Left behind, the women back home waited, their dread hidden
behind a mask of seeming indifference. Life would go on. People
would go about their business. No one need know. But there was
no escaping the assault on Walkerton. Clothes seemed to age with
every wash. Fabric that escaped the ravages of bleach succumbed
to the onslaught of chlorine. Their out-of-town grandchildren
were reluctant to visit and became uneasy in their apartment when
they did. Rita felt as if the community itself, the little town she
loved, had been ravaged and beaten, and she despaired, quietly,
away from prying eyes. But the anguish engulfed her husband,
Terry. The same indescribable sorrow he felt when he lost his
daughter and grandson in a horrific car crash more than a decade
earlier reappeared from nowhere. An unwelcome demon of gut-
wrenching mournfulness had returned with a vengeance, set
loose by the water crisis. He constantly felt on the verge of tears.
When the death of Maurice (Rocket) Richard, the famous Montreal
hockey player of a bygone era, displaced the E. coli disaster as

the top news story, the tears came at last. But the grief that flowed down Terry's cheeks was really for Walkerton. Whenever they could, the couple fled the town for the refuge of their sailboat, where they could shower or brush their teeth without hassle. In the end, the Halpins gave up looking for a house in the town they loved, the town in which they had planned to live out their lives. They moved instead fifteen kilometres north to Chesley, The Nicest Town Around, or so the welcome sign on the road says.

19

The Politics of Water

UNTIL THE Walkerton water crisis happened, the biggest
headache facing the Tory government in its second term in
the legislature was a scandal involving the government's real estate
arm, the Ontario Realty Corporation. Allegations of corruption
and mismanagement had surfaced. The Opposition suggested
there'd been bid-rigging during the sale of Crown lands to the
benefit of Tory supporters. The issue dominated daily question
period as the Liberals tackled the government, largely to no avail.
The story lacked pizzazz. It was complicated, difficult to follow,
and made for terrible television. In addition, while forensic audi-
tors were investigating, the government was able to parry demands
for information by insisting the probe be allowed to run its course.
Similarly, a complicated civil lawsuit against the government had
silenced most questions over the police killing of Dudley George
during the nighttime eviction of a group of aboriginal protesters
from Ipperwash Provincial Park on Lake Huron in September
1995. In the suit, George's family asserted Premier Mike Harris
himself had ignored top-level advice by directing police to use

force against the unarmed protesters, a claim the premier strenuously denied.

The Walkerton disaster hit the legislature like a lightning bolt. Coming as it did during a weeklong recess allowed the Opposition to prepare for a major offensive: Walkerton would be Mike Harris's Waterloo and they girded for bloody political battle. Already information was surfacing about problems in the Environment Ministry's oversight of the town's water. Pointed accusations were levelled about the changes the Tories had made in 1996 to the water-testing system as they took their axe to the bureaucracy. The ministry had also known about adverse water results in the town in the months and weeks leading up to the crisis but had failed to alert the public health unit. The entire Common Sense Revolution, the neo-conservative platform that had first swept Premier Mike Harris to power in 1995, was now on trial. Media interest was beyond intense. When the house resumed sitting May 29, a week after the first reports of illness in the stricken town, the Opposition, already inflamed by Harris's attempt to deflect blame to the previous New Democrats government, went on a blistering attack that would last for weeks. The session kicked off with Environment Minister Dan Newman proposing a motion to have an all-party legislative committee investigate the tragedy. The Opposition roared. Only a full-scale judicial inquiry as demanded by Concerned Walkerton Citizens would be sufficient, they argued. A grim Mike Harris refused outright.

"My experience with public inquiries is that they are very expensive, they take months to set up and get going, and we just think we need a legislative committee to get started right now," Harris told the legislature.

The proposal for a legislative committee, quickly dubbed a kangaroo panel by the Liberals, was badly flawed. For one thing, it would be dominated by Conservatives. For another, it was to be led by a Tory member who'd been forced to resign his cabinet post amid a scandal involving tax evasion. Passions and emotions ran high in raucous sessions that had the Speaker struggling to keep under control. Again and again, the Opposition accused the premier of failing the people of Walkerton. Again and again, they demanded a full-scale public inquiry as the only way to get to the heart of the tragedy. Again and again, Harris was dismissive.

"I suggest to you, nothing is easier than saying, 'Oh, we'll turn it over to a judge and let him take whatever time he wants to take and hire all the lawyers and away we go,' but I think that's an abdication of our responsibility as legislators."

Veteran Liberal member Sean Conway stood up in the house:

"With a legislative committee that's going to be led by Steve Gilchrist and controlled, if behind the curtain, by the now government house leader, Mr. Sterling, who was through 1998 and 1999 the minister of the environment, who may very well be culpable, how can any of us, least of all you, Mr. Premier, accept that as anything other than a sham and, for important members of the community like the government house leader, an obvious and potential conflict of interest?"

Reporters swarmed cabinet ministers demanding to know what had gone wrong in Walkerton and why they were refusing to call an inquiry. Environment Minister Dan Newman, a hard-working partisan member of the legislature who had fallen into what the government had always considered a junior posting only two months earlier, stammered his way through media scrums like a fox cornered by the hounds. The Tories also had another problem in the form of one of their own: Bill Murdoch, the shoot-from-the-lip popular member from Bruce County. First elected in 1990 in an election that saw the New Democrats come to power and the Tories firmly relegated to the political wilderness, Murdoch had proven popular with his constituents. The bearded cattle trader easily won re-election in the Tories' sweep into office in 1995 and might have been seen as cabinet material had it not been for his stubborn, independent streak and penchant for criticizing the Vise-Grip in which the "pimply-faced Nancy's in the premier's office," as he called them, held on caucus members. He was well aware of the demands in Walkerton for a judicial probe. Even though he didn't believe budget cuts had anything to do with the tragedy, he figured the media would keep blaming the government without one. So when the Liberals formally proposed an inquiry, he made it clear he'd vote in favour. It was the last thing the battered Tories needed. With the vote on the motion set to go, Labour Minister Chris Stockwell, a proficient if theatrical performer from Toronto, moseyed over.

"You can't vote for this," Stockwell whispered to the recalcitrant member.

"But they're right, we have to do this," Murdoch insisted. "If you don't do a full inquiry in this thing, we'll never get out of this thing."

Party whip Frank Klees sidled over.

"Bill, I beg you, don't."

"What am I getting for it?" the cattle trader shot back.

"Don't worry, we'll look after you. I promise," said Klees.

Murdoch understood the rules of the game as well as anybody. He couldn't go against his own party on a recorded vote on such an important issue, no matter how justified the Opposition might have been.

"Okay. I'll take that," he said at last.

Minutes after the Tories crushed the Liberal motion, Harris himself went over.

"You voted the right way," the premier said without smiling.

Still, it was becoming clearer by the minute that something had to give. On the morning of May 31, Harris appeared to be cracking.

"We want to get to the bottom of this in a full and open way," he said heading into a weekly cabinet meeting. "A public inquiry would be one way. I think it would take a lot longer to get to the bottom of this. A legislative committee would be another far more effective way."

But when at the same hour, the provincial coroner announced they were now investigating the possibility of nine deaths from the poisonous water, Harris capitulated. He put out a brief press release announcing a public inquiry and left it to Attorney General Jim Flaherty to make the formal announcement. In the house, Harris was a no-show, a fact pointedly noted by an Opposition now trying hard not to gloat. But in classic Tory government fashion, before Flaherty got up, two other senior ministers did their utmost to do what the government had always done so well: push a couple of diversionary hot buttons. First Health Minister Elizabeth Witmer bashed the federal government, a favourite Tory sport, over cuts to health funding. Then Education Minister Janet Ecker played another favourite card when she tabled a bill to crack down on unruly school students. The diversions were futile and Flaherty rose to his feet.

"The premier has today announced that in order to get to the bottom of the Walkerton tragedy, the Ontario government will appoint a judge or a retired judge to a commission of inquiry under the Public Inquiries Act."

When asked why he'd changed his mind on calling the inquiry, Harris again pointed at the Opposition parties, saying he was worried they wouldn't cooperate in committee hearings. Within days, he would be blaming the disaster on "human error." And then he blamed the town for not taking advantage of government grants to fix its water problems, a statement for which he was pilloried when it turned out to have been wrong. It all sounded so feeble. A little more than a week after Harris's about-face, his attorney general announced that Ontario Court of Appeal Justice Dennis O'Connor, whose brother had been a judge in Walkerton and had approved Stan Koebel's divorce settlement, would lead what would become arguably the widest ranging public inquiry the country had ever seen. And Premier Mike Harris himself would have to answer to it.

20

City Suits and Civil Suits

I't's not every day a taxi shows up at Stonegate. It was around noon when a young woman in jeans, a reporter from the *Globe and Mail*, got out. Susan Bourette wanted to ask a few questions about the source of the E. coli now known to have come from Well 5, which lay behind a bit of scrub just east of the Biesenthal property. The tall vet seemed reserved but friendly enough. Beyond having heard that E. coli found in his cattle were a near match to those found in the poisonous water, no one had told Dave Biesenthal anything.

"How would you feel if this farm was the origin of the contamination?" Bourette asked.

Biesenthal could feel his blood starting a slow boil. Her tape recorder suddenly felt like a weapon.

"I know this could potentially be the origin of the problem," he said. "But what can I do about it? Go out and shoot my cows? It's easy to say this is the origin, but how did it get from here to the well? I didn't take a bucket of manure and throw it down the well."

In London early the next morning, Laryssa was preparing for the Olympic team rowing trials when she heard her farm home had become national news. She raced for the phone and called her unsuspecting parents. It was 7 A.M.

"Why is our name all over the radio?" she asked a startled Carolyn. "Are you okay?"

It was as if a hand grenade had been tossed into the quiet farmhouse, heralding a hostile invasion of reporters, photographers, and TV cameramen. Biesenthal parked a front-end loader across the bottom of the long drive to dam the stream of intruders. He retreated to the far end of his farm to bale straw to get away from it all. His farm, his refuge, his home, soon began to feel like a cage surrounded by predators. Carolyn was constantly close to tears, no longer even wanting to go to church in town. Dave didn't feel much better. The market for his animals sagged.

"Those goddamn Toronto media are ruining this town," someone at the Becker's said to him.

The woman behind the counter gave him a rose. "For your wife," she said.

Some time after, a client from out of town was at the clinic. "I'm surprised they didn't lynch you," he said.

No. But it felt that way, a feeling reinforced with each visit from yet another of the dozens of investigators who arrived to prod him with questions about his manure, sample his cattle, or poke holes in his fields.

The car nosed through the opening between two small stone walls, a ceramic plaque with a B on the left, another with a black horse on the right. It edged up the well-tended gravel drive that runs from the highway between rows of small spruce and locus trees that form the edging of two fields of corn and beans. When he reached the top of the drive, a barn and small pasture to the right, the yellow-brick farmhouse to the left, the driver stopped. Biesenthal, who was standing in front of the stable, didn't recognize the car or driver, a shortish man neatly dressed in shirt and slacks in his mid-thirties. The stranger seemed thoroughly ill at ease. Biesenthal stalked over, his fists clenched.

"Who the hell are you? What the hell do you want?" he roared.

"I'm Peter Raymond," the man stammered, his eyes misting over. "My daughter passed away from E. coli. We just wanted to tell you we don't hold you responsible for her death."

When Carolyn pulled up a little while later, the visitor had just left.

"What's the matter now?" she asked her husband.

"Guess who was here," he said softly, tears streaming down his face.

Not long after the Biesenthals returned from a welcome break in Sydney where Laryssa had again made them proud with another Olympic bronze medal, Dr. Murray McQuigge presented his final report on the outbreak. In all, an estimated 2,300 people fell ill from the bad water in Walkerton. At least half, 1,286 people, lived in the town itself, 26 per cent of its entire population. The others worked or went to school in town, or, like little Mary Rose Raymond, had been among a stream of visitors on or around the Mother's Day weekend. About 725 people had passed through the Walkerton emergency room in the last two weeks of May, more than double the average number of ER visits. The worst day had been May 24, when 113 people had filed through. In all, the outbreak killed seven people: four died from E. coli O157 poisoning, three from the combined effects of E. coli and campylobacter bacteria. Had a calamity of this relative magnitude hit a city such as New York or Paris, 4 million people would have fallen ill in the space of two weeks and 14,000 would have died. Unimaginable, nuclear-bomb-scale catastrophe. McQuigge also reported that genetic mapping had determined the E. coli O157:H7 found in the town's tap water had come from a farm next to Well 5, known from Day 1 to be vulnerable to contamination. The bacteria had apparently found their way from the fields into the underground aquifer that fed the well. A day after McQuigge's report, a man in a suit arrived at Stonegate and

handed the Biesenthals a brown envelope. Stan Koebel and the
Walkerton Public Utilities Commission had named the couple as
third-party defendants in a $350-million class-action lawsuit.

The class-action lawsuit, launched at the height of the disaster,
was destined from the start to become much more than a legal
battle. Almost immediately, the already severely stressed town
split into factions over the wisdom of what amounted to suing
themselves. Nice people don't go around suing each other, some
said. It will bankrupt the municipality, others insisted. Retired
lawyer Terry Halpin, who for a few days had thought he was dying
from a mysterious illness, had launched the initial proceedings.
Halpin was primarily angry at the seemingly hit-and-miss
approach taken to informing the public about the boil-water
advisory. When one of the town's minor-league sports teams won
a championship, the occasion was celebrated by an impromptu
parade of fire trucks driving through town honking their horns
and sounding their sirens. Halpin believed that every available
police car, ambulance, and fire truck should have been out with
sirens blaring, warning the people. Given the size of the town,
they could have covered every corner in ten minutes flat. Instead,
word of the boil-water advisory had been left to percolate through
the town and beyond, leaving many to continue drinking the
potentially lethal bacteria cocktail. Halpin also believed that
because it was a Walkerton problem, any lawsuit should be homegrown. It was a fond hope. Soon, the town would find itself
stretched in a high-stakes legal tug-of-war between big-city
lawyers and the provincial government.

One of those city lawyers was Harvey Strosberg, a large man
with vast experience in class-action suits and dealing with government. Ultimately, Strosberg would spearhead a suit that came
to involve six law firms and dozens of lawyers, who together
demanded general and punitive damages of $350 million from the
municipality, the Walkerton Public Utilities Commission, Stan
Koebel himself, the health unit, and the Ontario government.
The lead plaintiff was Jamie Smith, a history teacher at Sacred

Heart, whose son's bout with E. coli poisoning in May 2000 was a terrifying reprise of a 1998 episode in which the child contracted the illness during an unexplained outbreak at a Walkerton day care. Provincial police Const. Jamie McDonald was a strong backup plaintiff.

From the outset, Strosberg realized that politics would determine how the class-action lawsuit would play out. What he didn't realize, perhaps somewhat naively, is just how intransigent the province would be. The tainted-water tragedy had quickly overtaken the political agenda, throwing the entire government and its ideology on the defensive. The Tories were in critical need of some brownie points on Walkerton. Their answer was the "compassion initiative," as they dubbed it, its purpose two-fold: to score those points and to cut the fledgling class action off at the knees. To Attorney General Jim Flaherty, it made perfect political sense. The government would do something voluntarily for Walkerton without any admission of fault. Its response would be driven by compassion rather than by legal or financial considerations. Under the no-fault plan Flaherty hatched, people in Walkerton could claim financial compensation for illness or the death of a loved one without having to go the tortuous court route.

"This isn't about legal liability, it's the right thing to do," Premier Mike Harris said. "The people of Walkerton should not have to go to court to get the help they need."

Outside town hall in early summer, a small group of Concerned Walkerton Citizens, among them Jamie Smith's wife, Stephanie, waited on the sidewalk for a meeting to end so they could ask Flaherty some questions. But when he emerged and the residents approached him, Bill Murdoch tried to steer him away. Although his Bruce-Grey-Owen-Sound riding had voted solidly Conservative, Murdoch had convinced himself that Walkerton was hostile political territory. He had already raised eyebrows in the town with his pronouncements immediately after Premier Mike Harris had visited back in May.

"That woman and a bunch of agitators were bussed in from thirty-five miles away," Murdoch had opined to a radio station minutes after Veronica Davidson had shouted after Harris. "The same bunch that's bussed around whenever Harris makes an election campaign stop."

The more the media and town questioned whether Harris's policies had played a role in the disaster, the more Murdoch dug in his heels. And the more Concerned Walkerton Citizens pressed for answers from the province, the more Murdoch tried to marginalize them with an antipathy that was visceral.

"It's getting late," Murdoch said as the group on the sidewalk attempted to talk to Flaherty.

"We don't care how late it is," someone said. "Lose some sleep."

While some of the group talked to Flaherty, Stephanie Smith watched from one side. A young aide to the minister came over and made some small talk.

"You know, you guys should get T-shirts, just like after the ice storm, that say, 'I survived the E. coli disaster.' "

Smith wanted to slap her but said nothing.

More than six seemingly endless months after he had issued the boil-water advisory at the height of the crisis, Dr. Murray McQuigge pronounced the tap water again safe to drink. It had been a mind-bogglingly painstaking process. Five kilometres of water mains had been replaced, a state-of-the-art filtration system installed at Well 7, while Wells 5 and 6 had been permanently decommissioned, the former more than a decade too late. The plumbing in each of the town's 1,816 buildings had been disinfected more than once, and thousands upon thousands of samples had been taken and scrutinized for any signs of contamination. In all, it had cost about $15 million.

"I'll come right to the point. I'm going to lift the boil-water advisory for Walkerton," McQuigge said to a round of applause from the several dozen townsfolk who'd braved a brutal snowstorm for the occasion.

Up front, about a dozen town and other officials, including Mayor Dave Thomson, lifted glasses of water to their lips and ostentatiously took a sip.

"This day has been so long in coming that it almost feels anti-climactic," McQuigge went on. "It may be anti-climactic, but it is a serious step in getting this town back to normal."

"Today's announcement means a gigantic burden has been lifted off our shoulders," Mayor Dave Thomson was saying. "Today is a day for optimism."

But there was little evidence of celebration. Around town, people collectively shrugged and carried right on drinking bottled water. The experts might have exorcised the killer bacteria but not the demons of fear and mistrust that haunted the town. And it was that mistrust that the class-action lawyers harnessed. At first blush, Flaherty's compensation plan was a political master-stroke that would put the class-action lawyers out of the Walkerton business. But it was also doomed from the start. For one thing, acceptance of a settlement under the plan meant waiving all further rights to sue. That's not unusual in the world of out-of-court settlements, but to a mistrustful citizenry, it was unacceptable. There were still people ill, children with seri-ously uncertain prospects, businesses on their heels. From the plaintiffs' perspective, the plan put the wolf in control of com-pensating the chickens for the henhouse he'd just ravaged. While the lawyers were confident their suit had all the merits needed to succeed, they realized the real battle would be fought, at least initially, in the public-relations arena. People would vote with their feet. If they opted in droves for the government plan, the class action would be dead in the water. Strosberg hired an Ottawa-based research firm to conduct a series of focus groups in the town. The results were stark, if unsurprising: more than 80 per cent of the people said they trusted the courts, less than 15 per cent the government. From there, it was a no-brainer to come up with a message the lawyers would deliver in every contact with the people they sought to represent: "Whom do you trust? Do you trust Mike Harris or do you trust the courts?"

Still, Strosberg figured this was a case that could be settled fairly painlessly if the government chose to cooperate, but his attempt at negotiation was unceremoniously rebuffed. The com-bative Flaherty, an ambitious lawyer-turned-politician with hardline conservative views, was not about to be told what to do by a bunch of class-action lawyers, especially not by Strosberg, who'd once embarrassed him in front of others at a top-level meeting. But in making a decision that would only serve to drive the legal bills into the many millions of dollars, Flaherty appeared to have seriously underestimated the mistrust the Harris government faced in Walkerton. Perhaps he had badly overestimated the people's desire for quick cash. Or possibly, he imagined the government could rely on its highly effective public-relations machine to turn opinions around. The government saturated the area with letters and ads extolling its plan, while taking various technical positions to delay the class-action proceeding for as long as possible. But at every turn, the class-action lawyers countered with their simple question: "Whom do you trust? Do you trust Mike Harris or do you trust the courts?"

Jamie Smith knew whom he could trust. Despite all the touchy-feely stuff coming from Flaherty's office about doing the right thing, it was open war. For more than eight gruelling hours in Toronto in early January, the government's lawyers dredged through every nuance and word of his affidavit, trying to discredit him in any way possible. They got nowhere. Finally, as required under Ontario law, a hearing to certify the class-action suit was scheduled before Superior Court Justice Warren Winkler. As it had done for months, the government argued its compensation plan was the preferred way to proceed. But it also had a curious backup argument: if the court were to decide the government had played a role in the deaths and illness in Walkerton, its lawyers argued that it was the result of a policy decision that made it immune to a lawsuit under well-established legal principles.

Justice Winkler listened quietly to the arguments, but on the second day, he became more interventionist, more challenging, more skeptical. He had heard enough. He called the bevy of lawyers together and floated the idea of mediating a settlement. What followed were days of intense and difficult negotiations. Winkler put on a virtuoso performance in the search for compromise.

Strosberg held out three conditions for a settlement. Court supervision was key. But he also realized there had to be something that gave people an immediate return: a minimum payment. He was also of the view that the government had run up the legal bill by its intransigence. So a third condition was complete payment of the legal fees but not, as is usual, from the final compensation award. At last it appeared a deal was in hand and the representative plaintiffs were told to assemble in Toronto. The courts would supervise the settlement. Every man, woman, and child in Walkerton would get at least $2,000 tax-free, more if their circumstances warranted. There would be no limit. The various insurance companies would kick in $17 million to cover the compensation and another $5 million for legal fees to end the action against their clients, among them Stan Koebel and the Biesenthals. In return for not having the action certified against it, the government agreed to foot the bill for any higher costs.

Companies facing litigation make a simple decision: What makes the most business sense? But government, with its massive resources, bases its decisions on a far fuzzier rationale: What makes good political sense? And what made good political sense to the Tory government was that its own Walkerton compensation plan had to be seen as the centrepiece of any class-action settlement. Strosberg was more than happy to give the government its due. And then a bombshell hit. A Canadian Press reporter uncovered details of the deal and the story hit the front pages. The article quoted a source who suggested the tentative deal showed just how poor Flaherty's "original" plan had been. The government threw a fit. There was no way it was going to guarantee an open-ended financial package if it couldn't take the political credit.

"We can't trust you guys," government lawyer Paul Morrison told Strosberg. "The leak had to come from your side."

"It didn't," said a stunned Strosberg. "I swear to you it wasn't me."

For the next two days, both sides haggled mistrustfully over every word of the press release that would announce the settlement, and every word of the public statement Strosberg would

make after the announcement. The government was sure
Strosberg would embarrass it in public. Strosberg was sure the
government would try to say the settlement was just a warmed-
over version of Flaherty's own plan, that he and his legal colleagues
had fought it in court simply to run up their own meters. To
ensure that didn't happen, Strosberg demanded Flaherty take the
stage with him at a news conference planned for after the pres-
entation of the proposed settlement to Judge Winkler.

"Bring Flaherty, I want Flaherty," he told Morrison.

"Flaherty's never going to come," Morrison told him. "You're
a lawyer so why shouldn't there be another lawyer?"

"I'm not going to stand there with a lawyer. I represent a class
and I want somebody who represents the government," Strosberg
insisted.

And so they haggled, even as the judge and assembled media
were kept waiting. At the ensuing nationally televised news
conference, Jamie Smith choked back tears as he praised the
agreement wholeheartedly and urged everyone in Walkerton to
accept it. Sitting to his left at the table next to each other were
Strosberg and the government's lawyer, Paul Morrison. You'd
have thought they were best buddies. Flaherty, of course, was a
no-show. The following night, hundreds of people jammed the
community hall in Walkerton to hear Strosberg and his fellow
lawyers extol the settlement. It was the largest turnout for any
meeting related to the calamity. No one in Walkerton questioned
the wisdom of the class action. Terry Halpin felt thoroughly vindicated. Three weeks later, Jim Flaherty was named deputy
premier and given the coveted finance portfolio.

21

Trial by Public Inquiry

N CRITICIZING public inquiries as a cumbersome, ineffective, and seemingly never-ending process, Premier Mike Harris might have misjudged one key factor: the man chosen to lead it, Dennis O'Connor. Although possessed of a powerful legal mind and a capacity for hard work, it would be his gentle sense of humour and unfailing courtesy that would endear him to the people of Walkerton and to those who appeared before him. His unstinting determination and fairness would quickly put the lie to New Democrat Leader Howard Hampton's ugly aspersion that the judge could not be trusted to probe a labour-unfriendly Conservative government because he had once represented a client in a case that attacked a fundamental tenet of Canadian unionism.

The Ontario Appeal Court justice set to work immediately after being named to lead the probe by assembling a formidable array of talent: Paul Cavalluzzo, a labour lawyer with expertise in public, constitutional, and administrative law; Brian Gover, a criminal lawyer and former Crown prosecutor; and Freya Kristjanson, a lawyer with already extensive experience in inquiries who drove to the first meeting with O'Connor with a broken hand.

It was a rainy Sunday in Toronto, June 2000, when they got together for the first time to tackle the mammoth task. There was so much to decide, from mundane questions such as what to call the probe (The Walkerton Inquiry) to more difficult issues of how to go about getting the information they needed and how to proceed. It was clear they needed seasoned help for their fact-finding. They determined that only investigators from the federal Royal Canadian Mounted Police would be seen as independent and above reproach. The initial request for documents went out in late June, barely six weeks after the first funerals. More than two dozen search warrants were drawn up and executed. Ultimately, as many as one million government documents would be turned over from eight ministries, along with a handful from the cabinet and premier's offices. Never before would a government's inner workings be subject to such intense public scrutiny.

Among the inquiry's first orders of business was to find out whether the town would be amenable to a visit by O'Connor, who wanted a first-hand look at the crisis. Cavalluzzo and Kristjanson drove up in early July. With them was irrepressible media guru Peter Rehak, a former long-time executive producer with CTV's national current affairs program *W5*, who firmly believed there's no point throwing a party if no one shows. There they found a citizenry imbued with a deep distrust of government officials and a cynicism about the media, which had rushed in at the height of the tragedy and rushed out as soon the story began to age. Yet people were open to an O'Connor visit and informal hearings were scheduled so as not to conflict with the bingo evenings at the Knights of Columbus hall just south of town.

On July 25, more than two months after she first fell ill with diarrhea and tested positive for campylobacter infection, Evelyn Hussey became the seventh death of the outbreak. Although she'd had heart trouble and had been terribly ill, she appeared to be recovering, had even walked around a little. Then her kidneys failed. She died just shy of her eighty-fifth birthday in Walkerton hospital, a day before O'Connor arrived in town.

For several days, residents poured out their grief, their anger, their questions. They came as well to private meetings, to share with the judge their stories of illness and death. O'Connor listened attentively to each and every one, occasionally asking a question or interjecting a word of encouragement, occasionally wiping a tear from his own cheek. It seemed as if the giant beating heart of the town had broken under the crushing weight of its grief. It was, as Pastor Beth said, as if the town somehow trusted O'Connor to put it back together again.

Provincial police, too, had thrown themselves into a criminal investigation and complained regularly the public inquiry was getting in their way by seizing documents and talking to witnesses. RCMP Insp. Craig Hannaford, the lead investigator for the inquiry, did his best to smooth provincial police feathers.

"We certainly won't be interfering with your investigation," Hannaford said over lunch one day to Insp. Paul Chayter, the provincial officer in charge of the criminal investigation.

"You being here interferes with my investigation," Chayter shot back.

Nevertheless, armed with a mandate from the highest level of government, the inquiry lawyers pressed on. Gradually, painstakingly, they began piecing together the bits of a giant jigsaw puzzle, and in late August, one of the centrepieces fell into place.

Lawyers defending the utilities commission against the class-action suit had begun to suspect all was not as it seemed as they struggled to unravel the tangled history of the water utility. At last it became clear to them that Stan and Frank had been falsifying the records. They passed that information to Bill Trudell and Ken Prehogan, who was acting for the PUC at the inquiry.

"I need to come in and see you," Trudell told Paul Cavalluzzo.

He took with him Prehogan, who, like Trudell, had been stunned by the revelations. Never had he come across a fraud case that didn't have a financial motive, pure and simple greed as its underpinning. Together, they met Cavalluzzo and Brian Gover in the third week of August and handed over a letter Prehogan had written indicating that the well records maintained by the Koebel brothers were unreliable. So were the sampling submission sheets. Therefore the test results themselves were not reliable, at least not in terms of where the samples were taken. The door was barely shut when Cavalluzzo and Gover looked at one another.

"Holy shit!" Cavalluzzo said. "Holy shit."

Until that meeting, the inquiry lawyers had assumed that what had happened was likely the result of inadvertence or incompetence at the local level. But the revelations of falsification had taken the probe into a whole new realm. It was obvious that if criminal charges were going to be laid, Stan and Frank were targets. Still, their stories were crucial. But getting the truth from Stan was proving difficult. These were events he dearly wished had never happened, events he wanted to forget. Deeply depressed, he was often confused and had trouble explaining himself. Gently but persistently, the inquiry lawyers worked to gain his and Trudell's confidence, so that ultimately, the people of Walkerton would hear from the man they had trusted for so long to look after their drinking water. He owed it to them.

Frank, too, had become increasingly agitated. The various lawyers were pressing back into the past, into the Ian McLeod era, and he was greatly troubled. On two occasions, Frank showed up unexpectedly at Ruth McLeod's home, once with his wife.

"If Ian was still there, this would never have happened," he told McLeod's widow. "Now we've got this three-ring circus in Walkerton."

It seemed as if he were trying to warn her, as if he wanted her to be prepared. The lawyers were advising him to say there were "irregularities" in how her husband had run the PUC, that he hadn't trained them properly to do the job. Ruth was struck by his use of the word "irregularities." That didn't sound much like Frank talk. As she watched him pace nervously, she tried to figure out why he'd come to visit. Then it hit her. They were going to try to shift the blame onto her husband, who had died in 1993 of a brain aneurysm and couldn't defend himself.

"That's not right," Ruth said.

"I know that," Frank said.

"You should do what's right," she said. "Tell the truth."

"I feel really bad," said Frank, his distress evident. "I had so much respect for Ian. I miss him."

Don Herman, the retired PUC backhoe operator, was also surprised when Frank showed up at the door of his trailer-home just west of Hanover. Hermy thought his visitor looked like hell as he paced the kitchen floor. Frank looked like a kid who has done something wrong and is scared his dad will find out and lay on a beating when he gets home from work.

"Al Buckle is shooting his mouth off all over town," Frank said.

Hermy had no idea what Frank was talking about.

"If people come in here asking you questions about what was going on down at the PUC shop, don't you tell them nothing," Frank suddenly said.

"There's been nobody in yet," Herman replied, still puzzled.

Frank continued mumbling to himself as he walked around in tight circles. He said something about Stan being in trouble of some kind, that they wouldn't even let the two of them talk to each other. And then, as unexpectedly as he'd arrived, he left again. Herman felt vaguely threatened. What exactly had Frank been trying to tell him? He's running scared, he decided.

"What did Frank want?" Herman's wife asked.

"He just wanted to tell me to keep my mouth shut."

On October 16, 2000, the TV satellite trucks and other media vehicles rolled into town once again. Reporters patrolled outside the post office, or trolled Main Street looking for someone, anyone, to interview. It was time for the inquiry's public hearings to begin. At last, the real answers would come. The hearings opened with technical experts who talked in great detail about the weird and wonderful world of hydrogeology, about scrubbing pipes, about chlorine residuals, about surface water and groundwater. This wasn't news. This was education. For the media, who had played such a pivotal role in alerting the world to the disaster and had posed so many questions about political accountability, it was as exciting as watching paint dry and most left. But stitch by stitch, as transcripts and exhibits piled up, the inquiry lawyers began creating an intricate tapestry of the Walkerton disaster. After the experts, a parade of Environment Ministry officials from Owen Sound testified. With the exception of Michelle Zillinger, they all sounded much the same, as if they were part of some alien system populated by paper-pushers where decisive action and strong opinions were neither wanted nor needed. Whatever had been going on at the PUC, the ministry had let it go on. In town, people who had always believed that Stan Koebel wasn't solely to blame felt vindicated. But it was Mayor Dave Thomson's turn on the stand that provided the first moments of drama. Asked how he felt when he finally accepted the truth of Dr. McQuigge's allegations about Stan Koebel, Thomson gasped audibly and began sobbing into his hands. Watching the proceedings on TV, Frank Koebel suddenly felt stabbing pains in his chest. He thought he was having another heart attack.

It was the first time since the hearings had begun six weeks earlier that the raw emotions stirred by the tragedy had bubbled so clearly to the surface. The elderly man who ruled council with a thinly gloved iron fist cut a sorry figure as he tried to explain himself. Why, for example, hadn't he declared a state of emergency? It was a question many townspeople wanted answered.

"We felt that we had it under control and we wished to make sure that the water got looked after right, and had the experts there to do it," he said.

But he could provide no answers for his own apparent indifference to the unfolding crisis. He had simply done his best to handle a situation in which he'd been as blindsided as anyone. He was unable to recall specific details about many events and, in his evident nervousness, fractured the English language:

"I knew what E. coli was as far as hamburger, those sorts of eating, with meats. But I wasn't aware of E. coli in water, no. Not that it was detrimental in water."

During a recess, Thomson stood outside in the chilly November sunshine, his face flushed, shaking like a leaf as he tried to light a cigarette. There wasn't a trace of a smile or even comprehension when a reporter told him what had befallen his big-city counterpart: Toronto's colourful Mayor Mel Lastman had just set the provincial capital a-titter with his announcement he was being sued by his long-time former lover and the two children he fathered by her for $6 million. Thomson's day of testimony had been relegated to secondary news. And then it was time for the lowest man on the totem pole to testify.

Poor Al Buckle: hired to cut the grass, not corners; bubble-checker without peer; first-rate ditchdigger, even in his good clothes; Frank Koebel's helper as of March 2, 1992.

"Now, as you know, that bubble was not meant to be used to determine the chlorine residual," Cavalluzzo noted at the inquiry in early December.

"I always believed that was the way they done it. That's my believing: that's the way it was done," Buckle responded.

"Right. Did you ever question Frank as to why he didn't use the tool kit that had the purpose of determining the chlorine residual?"

"No, I never did."

"Did you ever use the tool kit itself?"

"Occasionally. But, my judgment on the colours would never match to Frank's colours."

Around the inquiry room, lawyers in expensive suits stifled grins.

"And I wasn't that familiar with it. It just didn't work right for me. So I'd watch when he set the bubble and whatever the bubble was, that's what I would go by."

Like his mentor, Buckle didn't much care for chlorinated water. And like so many others, he was spectacularly, blissfully unaware of its importance.

"I thought the water was good because every different occasion we were at the pumphouse, we'd drink the water out of the raw side," he told Cavalluzzo.

"Why is that?"

"It's nice and cold, clear and clean, and tastes good."

"What did the chlorinator do? What was it supposed to do?"

"Put chlorine in to kill the bugs."

"And what bugs was the chlorinator there to kill?"

"Just some bugs or whatever was in the water."

From Buckle's testimony, it became increasingly clear that what had been going on at the PUC was more than simple oversight, more than simple sloppiness. Frank had directed him to mislabel water samples, orchestrated a system in which critical guidelines were ignored, where expediency took precedence over safety concerns, where records were falsified or simply invented. Rows and rows of numbers were entered on dozens of log sheets that, ultimately, were meaningless. And in the tragedy that was Walkerton, Al Buckle learned a valuable, if belated, life lesson:

"You do what you're told, but to what I know now, how danger the water is, I would have definitely stated that I don't feel comfortable in doing it and I'm not going to do it your way any more. I would have questioned him."

But the truly disturbing picture emerged only when Frank testified. Dressed uncomfortably in a black suit perhaps more appropriate for a funeral, the burly foreman tried to explain the seemingly inexplicable. He held back nothing as he described drinking on the job, the routine falsification and fudging of the records, the deliberate mislabelling of samples, and the attitude that prevailed at the PUC that chlorination and adherence to ministry guidelines just weren't that important. He said Stan knew about it, participated in the falsifications, and suggested they'd learned the way of doing business from their former manager, a drunken Ian McLeod. At times, Frank's pudgy fingers would rise to his face and rub his wet eyes. But he kept on going, kept baring his soul.

"Did you ever think it was wrong or inappropriate to enter fictitious numbers into the operating sheets?" Brian Gover asked.

"I would say it wasn't completely correct I was to be doing that, yes."

"If you had some concerns about whether it was an appropriate practice to do those things, my question to you is: Why did you do them?"

"Because I didn't have the time to dedicate to the situation."

"Did you ever raise that time constraint concern with Stan Koebel or anybody else?"

"He was in the same situation I was."

Frank Koebel left the inquiry building surrounded by three police officers for protection. But there was no lynch mob. There were no angry protesters, only a few photographers wanting one last shot. It looked more like he was under arrest. In Walkerton, a stunned community felt as if the town had been crucified.

A few days later, as Brian Gover stood in line for his early-morning coffee at Tim Hortons, an older man buttonholed the not yet quite awake lawyer.

"You that fella on the TV?" he asked, his face a breath away from Gover's.

"I am with the inquiry," allowed Gover, as he tried in vain to put a little more distance between himself and the crotchety stranger.

"Well, I've got a complaint," the man said. "There's too much damn chlorine in the water."

While everyone now wanted to hear from Stan Koebel, it was Dave Patterson who got to testify next at the inquiry.

The public had always been led to believe that it was Dr. Murray McQuigge who had been the hero of the moment in issuing the boil-water advisory, yet Patterson's actions were of more critical importance. It was he who had done so much to track down the E. coli in the water. It was he who had spoken to Stan Koebel about the water and who finally recommended and drafted the boil-water advisory. For the better part of three full days on the stand, he recounted in detail those gruelling, seemingly endless hours and days that had begun with Dr. Kristen Hallett's call on the Friday of the May long weekend.

Of all the lawyers in the room, perhaps the one paying the most attention to Patterson's words was Bill Trudell. More than any other witness, possibly even more than Frank, it was Patterson who held out the potential for providing the most damaging evidence against Stan. It was on Patterson's word that

McQuigge had pointed the finger at his client, had repeatedly told
the world how Stan had withheld the information about the bad
test results, reassured them the water was safe while the health
unit frantically sought answers and hundreds of people fell ill. So
while McQuigge had been the face and voice of the accusation
against Stan Koebel, it was Patterson who was the source of that
accusation. When it was time to cross-examine the grey-haired
assistant director of health protection, the attention level rose
several notches. Trudell went at Patterson with quiet fury and
indignation. His forehead furrowed, he glared at the witness
above his square-rimmed glasses. He seemed to summon every
angel in the universe to his side.

"All right," Trudell began, his voice dripping disgust. "You're
under oath and I'll get to it now: You find somewhere in your
notes where Stan Koebel ever said to you that the water is fine
or that he ever reassured you that the water was fine, or that he
ever said it was safe or he ever said it was secure, before you and
Dr. McQuigge went public and said that he said it."

He paused, as if awaiting a confession, an admission. And then
he went on, his voice resonating like a preacher, its tone growing
in accusatory emphasis with every word.

"Where did he say it? He didn't, Mr. Patterson. He never said
it to you. Because it's not in your notes and it's not in your report
to the Ministry of the Environment. What you did is you attrib-
uted it to Mr. Koebel. And then you and Dr. McQuigge went
public. And you said he told you it was safe. He told you it was
secure. He assured you. And he never did it. And look what's happened since then?"

Patterson wasn't budging.

"What he did not do was share any of the knowledge that he
had," Patterson replied calmly and firmly. "As I said, the impression that I had every time that I talked to Stan Koebel was that
the water system was normal. There was nothing. I asked him,
'Is there any unusual events. Is there anything I should be aware
of?' He provided me with nothing."

Trudell wasn't about to give up. He sniffed loudly.

"And then you know what you did with Dr. McQuigge? You went on to issue press releases: 'The PUC has assured us from the start that the water supply was secure.' You let that out, didn't you? You destroyed Stan Koebel by saying these things."

The word "destroyed' seemed to hang in the air and fill the room.

"No," Patterson replied. "How many opportunities did he have to share the information that he had, to tell me that there was a problem? He did not do that."

It was high drama, spectacular even. It was breathtaking. But, ultimately, it was futile.

The aim of a judicial inquiry is not to ascribe blame or find fault. It is, at heart, a fact-finding exercise, a way of uncovering the truth about events as a prelude to making recommendations on how similar events can be avoided in the future. It does not punish except in the form of public exposure. There is no sentencing, no jail cell at the end of a long corridor waiting to swing shut with a deafening, metallic clang. And yet, for Stan Koebel in particular, the chair on which he sat might have been in a prisoner's box. Trial by public inquiry. A massive array of evidence already gathered. A verdict of guilty already pronounced in the court of public opinion. A newspaper cartoon – one of the gentler ones published at this time – showed Stan Koebel alongside that paragon of incompetence and sloth, Homer Simpson, with the simple caption: "Separated at birth?"

When Stan Koebel looked around the room that icy mid-December morning, camera flashes split the air while lawyers and spectators stared at him. Photographers contorted themselves, waiting for him to pick up the glass of water on the table in front of him and take a sip. He glanced around the room, resting his gaze for a brief moment on his family: his parents, Carole, Jacob, Stephanie. His psychiatrist sat unobtrusively to one side. Pastor Beth too. He flashed the briefest of winks at them. A wan, resigned smile flitted momentarily across his slips. He reached into a pocket and withdrew a handkerchief and blew his nose, a thunderous sound echoing through the microphone on the lapel of his black suit and out the large speakers into the expectant room. Then the cameras fell silent and the judge arrived. It was time. At the stroke of noon, Monday, December 18, 2000, the inquiry began hearing from its last witness of the year. Unlike with any other witness, it was Stan's own lawyer, Bill Trudell, who stood up first and began a gentle probing.

"Mr. Koebel, have you ever testified before?"

"No, I have not."

"And have you ever seen so many lawyers gathered around before in front of you?"

"No, I have not."

"They're all good people and they all have jobs to do, and so we're just going to start and go through it. Right?"

"Right."

Trudell asked a few simple questions: his age, his length of service at the PUC, what, briefly, he'd done there, letting him see a friendly face. Before they'd come in that morning, Stan had shown Trudell a statement that he and Carole had prepared.

"You told me that there's something that you wanted to say to the commission this morning. Is that right?" Trudell asked.

"That's correct."

"And before I go any further, you go ahead."

"Okay," Stan said. He looked down at a piece of paper and began reading in a soft, steady monotone. It was as if all other sound had been sucked out of the inquiry room by a giant vacuum.

"I'm not very good at words, so I wrote down a few things," he began.

"If I may read: Words cannot begin to express how sorry I am, and how bad I feel about the events leading up to, and including, the last seven months. I accept responsibility for my actions. I am one of the pieces of the puzzle that came together in May, and I am grateful for this opportunity to speak. Thank you."

For the first time since the E. coli disaster had struck the town, here was an apology, an admission of responsibility. Imperfect, perhaps, but an acknowledgement nonetheless. A simple but profound expression of remorse that few could doubt. Trudell paused a second or two to let the words sink in. Now the tough slogging would begin as the lawyer attempted to set the stage, to create the backdrop, to control the lighting, fading gently from pre-show darkness to a gentle, diffuse spotlight. He would get to the heart of the matter, to his client's heart, in only the most general of ways by going straight to the questions everyone wanted answers to.

"Now, Mr. Koebel, did you ever tell Mr. Patterson or Mr. Schmidt on May 19 or May 20 that the water was safe or the water was secure?"

"No, I did not."

"Mr. Koebel, when is the first time that you read the bad sample results in relation to the distribution system?"

"On Saturday, May 20."

"And where did you read them?"

"In my office."

"And where were they?"

"Under a pile of other papers and documents on my desk."

Stan Koebel had drawn a line in the sand beyond which he would not cross. He could and would admit to falsifying records and sloppy testing procedures, misleading the ministry and the utilities commissioners. As manager, he alone was ultimately responsible for those acts of omission and commission, which he chalked up to complacency. He could offer up a belated admission that he was spectacularly unqualified for the job he'd held for a dozen years. But how could he possibly admit to sitting on a report showing potentially lethal bacteria in the water even as people lay dying? How to face the fact that if he'd acted appropriately even one or two or three days earlier, scores, perhaps hundreds of people might have been spared the terrible torment and suffering of E. coli poisoning? How could he ever again face his neighbours? How could he ever face himself? And so he drew a line in the sand under which he buried the damning fax.

Trudell sat down. He'd barely taken ten minutes. Stan had dipped his toe into the scalding water and it had not burned. It was Brian Gover's turn to ask the questions. Frank Koebel Sr. sat erect, watching his son testify, his head and shoulders falling slightly with each revelation, finally slumping almost to his knees. He left the room and did not return. For two-and-a-half more days, Stan Koebel submitted to unrelenting scrutiny. With each break in the proceedings, photographers followed his every step, clicking away in what surely must have been among the all-time most photographed pee breaks in history. At lunch hour, Stan would disappear home to take medication, to escape the glare. Hour upon hour, he answered questions in a heavily sedated monotone, his replies just a few words. Steve Lorley could barely believe this was the same man who had been his tough-minded, demanding boss. At times Stan looked as if he'd collapse, but he held on, clinging to his reality.

"Mr. Koebel, you'd never flushed after an initial bad test before," Gover asked, his voice betraying a sympathy of which Bill Trudell might have been proud. "Is that right? You've told me that before?"

"That's correct."

"Isn't it true that those extraordinary efforts of the May long weekend are one of these two things: they're one of either a precautionary measure or an attempt to cover up a problem that you knew existed within the town's water system. It's one of those two isn't it, Mr. Koebel?"

"Yes, it is."

"Which one is it?"

"It was for precautionary measures."

The fog had proven impenetrable, even to the piercing lasers shone by some of the brightest legal talents in the business. Still, it made no sense. His explanation defied logic except perhaps as a flimsy fig leaf covering the most achingly pathetic shortcoming in his very sense of self. It was almost over and still Stan could not come completely clean. He had survived hours of examination, coming perilously close to, but never quite stepping over, the line. Not even when Earl Cherniak, representing Murray McQuigge and David Patterson, pulled and tugged on him with all the gentleness of a pitbull.

"They had called you because there were reports of sickness," Cherniak asked. "They wanted to know about the water system. Yes?"

"Yes, and I said I thought the water was okay."

"I mean, they would certainly take it that you meant that the water was safe, wouldn't they?"

"No, sir."

"They wouldn't take it that way?"

"No, I don't know how they took it, sir."

"But you understood that's why they were calling you, didn't you?"

"To see if the water was okay."

"To see if the water was okay?"

"Uh huh."

"Meaning safe?"

"No, to see if the water was okay."

"Well, is there a difference between the water being okay, sir, and the water being safe?"

"I think there's two variations to it, yes."

"Well, maybe you better explain to the commissioner what the difference is between safe water and okay water?"

"We knew we had adverse samples with 4/9 Highway and I wasn't sure if the system was intact or not. So if the water was of good quality or not."

"But you said it was okay?"

"I thought the water was okay."

Soon, it was all over. Stan Koebel had spoken, offered up his accounting of the tragedy that had occurred, had accepted some measure of responsibility, tried his best to explain the earthquake that had collapsed his world, leaving in its stead a mound of still smouldering rubble. This time, there would be no police escort from the building. There was, of course, no need. Instead, Gus van Harten, an aide to the inquiry, would be the getaway driver. But Van Harten was never trained to be a getaway driver. He'd forgotten to warm up the car that frozen December day, and so Stan sat helplessly trapped in the vehicle surrounded by photographers before van Harten could scrape the windshield clean and defrost the windows and they could flee in safety.

"How's he doing?" Trudell asked Carole Koebel a few hours later by phone.

"He got in the front door. He hit the couch and that's it," she responded.

Exhausted and drained of every last ounce of energy, Stan had escaped a mocking, hostile world into the blackness of sleep.

22

Severance

THE NATIONAL MEDIA that showed up for the Monday-night council meeting weren't there to listen in on discussions about zoning variances or complaints about tree-cutting or garbage pickup. On the agenda was an issue that perhaps more than any other had divided the community: Stan Koebel's $98,000 severance, agreed to by the virtually defunct public utilities commission days before the municipal election in November 2000. In the immediate aftermath of the crisis, Bill Trudell had successfully negotiated having Stan put on compassionate leave. But the revelations of the dangerous corner-cutting that Stan oversaw as manager darkened the picture. Still, Trudell insisted that firing Stan, who somehow wanted to believe he would wake up one morning and find out it was all a bad dream, would amount to cruel and unusual punishment. It would leave him in dire straits, perhaps shatter the last shred of self-respect he clung to, push him over the edge into an abyss from which no one returns. So Trudell made the case for Stan's resignation in exchange for financial recognition of both his twenty-eight years of service and his perilous state of mind. Although predisposed to help the man they knew as dedicated and industrious, the elected commissioners, Jim Kieffer and Richard Field, hedged. The optics were, to say the least, not good. Trudell pressed hard and, finally, everyone bought into the plan. The commissioners agreed to pay Stan for his unclaimed 99.5 days vacation plus another $64,000, almost a year's salary, in exchange for his resignation. It seemed the humane thing to do. And it sent shockwaves through the community and sparked anger across the country. But the utilities commission, which soon after divested itself of its electrical operations, had an embarrassing problem: it didn't have the money to pay him. So it asked the municipality to pick up the tab, dropping a political stick of dynamite into the small council chamber as reporters and TV cameras looked on.

Mayor Dave Thomson had figured he might have a way out of the pickle, a way to defuse the anger, or at least deflect it away from council. One of the newly elected commissioners, Warren Hawthorne, was in Port Elgin at work for Union Gas when he was paged. The mayor wanted to see him right away. Hawthorne drove back and went into a private meeting with Thomson. The two men exchanged pleasantries. Then Thomson hauled out a scrap of paper, scrawled something on it, and slid it across the desk without saying a word. On it was written $150,000.

"Can you use that to look after some of the PUC bills?" Thomson said.

"I'll have to think about it," a surprised Hawthorne said.

That night, Thomson told council that Hawthorne, who was not around to argue, had shown up in his office to ask for money for the PUC. The fuse on the explosive severance issue remained lit. In town, people who had wanted to believe that, somehow, the tragedy had occurred despite Stan's honest, best efforts, found themselves appalled by the notion that he would be rewarded. Some were surprised to learn he'd been earning $69,000 a year, not out of line for the position he'd held, but certainly a handsome salary in a town where many people earn little more than the minimum wage. Council was split. The two new councillors, Charlie Bagnato, manager of the Walkerton liquor store, and Chris

Peabody, teacher at Sacred Heart and part-time activist, opposed paying Stan. That left it to Councillor Steve Barker, a lawyer who lived outside town, to shore up their ranks. Barker was also adamant that Koebel should not get a penny beyond his absolute legal entitlement.

"I will not spit on the seven graves," said Barker in his distinctive drawl. "It's not sufficient to say he didn't mean to cause any harm. He did."

It was a good speech that clearly enjoyed the support of the non-media spectators. Councillor Audrey Webb, renowned in certain circles for her baked goods, waved her hands in agitation, trying to remember what she remembered. Deputy mayor Rolly Anstett looked at the mayor, trying to decide which way the wind was blowing. It was town lawyer Rod McLeod, whose own meter had already racked up millions in legal fees since the crisis hit, who saved the day or, at least, saved that night. While the municipality was obliged to pay Stan the $34,000 in outstanding vacation pay, McLeod said the rest of the severance agreement might not hold up because Stan hadn't revealed the full extent of his malpractice when he'd signed it. McLeod said he wanted to examine Stan's personnel file to see what the deal had been based on. But to do that, council needed to disband the PUC and take over what was left of it. That sparked objections from some residents, who felt that two new commissioners had just been elected and should oversee the town's water. Ignoring them amounted to an assault on democracy. Councillors floated the idea of having the water and sewage brought under the auspices of the town's works department.

"Why not?" taunted gadfly Phil Englishman. "It all tastes the same anyways."

Even the Queen appeared amused. But McLeod's opinion prevailed. At the end of the evening, the PUC no longer existed, ending a proud run of almost half a century. Stan Koebel would get his vacation money right away, but he'd have to wait several more months for the rest while McLeod, his meter still ticking, thumbed his way through the manager's previously unblemished personnel file looking for a loophole in the agreement. When Stan

Koebel sued the town for the balance of the money plus another $15,000 in punitive damages, council wilted in the face of a protracted and expensive legal fight of uncertain prospect. They voted to pay up, along with another $5,900 to cover his legal costs in fighting for his money. In return, Stan did accept a reduced severance of $48,000, rather than the $64,000 initially agreed to.

"It really hurts," said Englishman. "The bottom line is that Stan did not do his job."

News of council's decision prompted the *Toronto Star* to run an editorial cartoon showing Stan holding his cheque as he danced on a grave with seven crosses. It was powerful. It was vicious. Someone, somewhere, took it upon themselves to fax a death threat to Stan's new lawyer.

23

Humanity and Failure

June 29, 2001

ORE THAN A YEAR after his visit to Walkerton, Premier Mike Harris returned. This time, he would be under oath. Scores of people began lining up early, some getting up at the break of a hot sunny dawn, waiting to hear the premier answer to the judicial inquiry he had called so reluctantly twelve months earlier. Dozens of reporters and photographers descended on the inquiry building as satellite trucks again filled the parking spots in the biggest media crush since Stan Koebel had testified over three frosty December days. This time, there were real protesters, some from out of town, who chanted noisily as Harris was whisked into the small inquiry room ("We're wise to Mike Harris's lies"), some from Walkerton who stood silently behind placards (Mike Harris Is Killing Ontario). And then there was the protester who walked around with an anti-Harris sign until reporters hounded him into admitting he was really an undercover police officer. Standing quietly behind a sign with her mother was fifteen-year-old Nicole Longmire, a Grade 9 student at Walkerton District Secondary School and one of the many who had fallen ill from the contaminated tap water.

"I want him to admit that what happened was partly his fault," Nicole said. "It would be nice to hear him admit it, although it won't take away all the hurt that I had to live through."

The hard wooden surplus benches from the old Brampton courthouse were packed as Harris became the 107th witness and the first Ontario premier in more than half a century to testify before a judicial inquiry. But beyond a grim sense of satisfaction at seeing the province's top politician forced to swear on the Bible and sit in the seat once occupied by Stan Koebel, Harris's evidence offered little comfort for the people of Walkerton. In the days and weeks leading up to his testimony, documents put before the inquiry had revealed years of warnings from scientists and senior bureaucrats about the hazards of slashing the Environment Ministry almost in half. So, too, were there warnings about the confusion created by the rushed privatization of water-testing laboratories, implemented in just two months despite expert advice to phase it in over two or three years. Even a letter from the health minister to the environment minister calling for an immediate regulation to clarify the reporting protocol in the event a laboratory detected bad water had disappeared into a black bureaucratic hole. Two cabinet ministers had already testified that the various risks had been assessed and were deemed to be "manageable." Not a shred of paper among the million documents the government offered the inquiry showed any risk assessment was ever done.

"These reductions will have an adverse impact on the delivery of environmental protection service levels, which in turn will increase public health and safety risks," Paul Cavalluzzo quoted from one top-level ministry document.

"There's risks in everything," Harris replied. "But I can tell you at no time was it ever brought to cabinet's attention, to my attention, that the implementation of these [cuts] would cause increased risk to the health and safety of any citizens anywhere in the province."

"We've got document upon document upon document of increased risk to health and safety," Cavalluzzo countered.

"If I felt there was any risk and it had been brought to my attention, we would not have proceeded," Harris insisted.

In a familiar defence of his government's neo-conservative policies, the premier explained that his government had inherited a budget deficit of almost $11 billion that was bankrupting the province. Getting the public's fiscal house in order had to be his top priority, he argued.

"We felt the biggest risk to the people of Ontario was doing nothing."

Time and again he rejected the contention that his government's policies or procedures had any part in the tragedy. There would be no apology, no concession that, just maybe, his government might have, or ought to have, done anything differently, no acceptance of any responsibility of any kind.

"I'm accountable for any action, any policy that our government has taken," he said, choosing his words carefully. "I accept that accountability."

Under the circumstances, it was difficult to fathom just what the premier meant by accountability.

After more than five hours of testimony, Harris was quickly ushered down the front steps, through the crush of reporters and photographers, into the trademark minivan and was whisked away.

"I felt sick listening to him," said resident Joan Weiler.

After ten months, well over one hundred witnesses, hundreds of thousand of pages of documents, transcripts, and exhibits, the Walkerton inquiry was essentially over, although further searches of the premier's office would leave lingering questions about just what Harris might have had to hide. In its final submissions to O'Connor, the government, not surprisingly, denied any role of any description in what was one of the country's worst public-health disasters. It was, the province insisted, Stan Koebel's fault. That prompted an agitated Bill Trudell to deliver one of the best performances of his life as he lashed back at the government. His final impassioned words resembled that of a lawyer desperately

trying to persuade a jury to spare his client the noose as he
rejected the notion that Stan Koebel, by his wilful fraudulence,
had single-handedly brought the disaster upon both himself and
a trusting, unsuspecting town.

"It's not dishonesty, it's not cunning," Trudell said of Stan's
frantic, futile attempt to cope with the unimaginable catastrophe
that hit one long weekend in May.

"It is humanity, it is a failure."

Epilogue

T HE DAY IS RAW. In the town of Stratford, at one of the city's
busiest intersections, a man dressed in a heavy, bright
orange protective suit is perched atop a cherry picker wielding a
pair of wire-cutters through thick work gloves as he makes connections to a traffic light. A yellow hood covers his ears, the strap
pulled tightly under his bulging chin, the white hard hat he is
wearing blends into the sky. His face is ruddy from the cold, his
forehead revealing a crease of concentration.

"I'm happy to be working," says Stan Koebel.

The job does not last. In Walkerton, a For Sale sign swings
idly outside the modest bungalow at 902 Yonge Street. The asking
price is $64,000. Stan is packing his truck as he and Carole
prepare to leave town for good.

Frank Koebel remains on sick leave while lawyers haggle over
a permanent solution, but Dave Patterson has finally slipped
into retirement. Janice Hallahan, Bob McKay, and his PUC
buddies work for the new hydro utility where Tim Hawkins is
acting foreman. In Owen Sound, Kristen Hallett tends her
patients. Beth Conroy, exhausted by the months of spiritual crisis
in the town, is pastor at a church in St. Catharines. Walkerton's
Lutheran Church has a vacancy. The McDonalds are living in
London. Their family has grown by one. It takes eight months

for their house in Walkerton to sell to another resident, and then only after the price drops three times. The Hammells, too, are gone. They could not stand living on their street any more. Hanover is now home. Kody, like some two dozen other kids, still needs regular hospital checkups. He will likely need them for at least the next twenty years. His protein levels are consistently too high, a sign perhaps of permanent kidney damage. It makes him cranky. In his living room is a carved wooden angel. Many, many others still suffer lingering, unexplained after-effects of E. coli poisoning. Doctors tell a couple their young child will need a new kidney in the foreseeable future. The pregnant mother confides that she expects her still-to-be born baby will one day be the donor. Brad Smith has returned to live in Walkerton, to be closer to his daughters. In his wallet, he carries a folded newspaper picture of Tamara on the gurney. The newsprint is yellowing. He looks at it for comfort when life suddenly feels like hell again. On the anniversary of the disaster, families mourn the loss of their loved ones. The media return, keeping Bruce Davidson and Ron Leavoy of Concerned Walkerton Citizens busy. A permanent memorial garden has been planted off Yonge Street on what was a bare lawn in front of the county building. On the day the Governor General comes for the formal opening, "killer" appears on the sidewalk outside Stan's house before being quickly white-washed over. The media leave again. The town looks forward now. The Victorian-era buildings and houses seem to stand just a touch taller and prouder. There is a third traffic light. Newman's restaurant hums evenings and Rob's Sports Bar and Roadhouse is often packed late nights. Draft beer and other more exotic drinks are again served in glasses. Dave Thomson is firmly in charge of council, but Councillor Charlie Bagnato wins his battle to have "Brockton" painted over on the landmark north water tower and "Walkerton" painted back on. Main Street bustles in its small-town way. There is a movement afoot to split from Brant and Greenock. Wells 5 and 6 are plugged and abandoned. Well 7 supplies the water via a state-of-the-art filtration and chlorination system run by OCWA, for whom Al Buckle cuts the grass, not corners. Well 9 is under development as the search for another water source goes on. Sometimes, it hardly seems to matter. Many people still use bottled water.

Across the country, boil-water advisories proliferate. There have been as many as eight hundred by some counts. But who's counting? In Ontario, there are tougher new provincial drinking-water laws in effect. Critics dismiss them as inadequate without a comprehensive plan for protection, treatment, monitoring, and enforcement that ends with the tap but starts with the source, and billions of dollars in structural upgrades. Mike Harris worries even less about the naysayers. He is leaving politics anyway. A chill goes down Stephanie Smith's spine when she hears about a cryptosporidium outbreak in North Battleford, Saskatchewan, that causes dozens to fall ill after the parasite finds its way from the city's sewage plant into the drinking water system downstream. The filter that should have caught the bugs wasn't working properly but no one alerted residents, who are split over the wisdom of a class-action lawsuit. A judge there consults Dennis O'Connor on how to run a public inquiry.

The direct costs of the Walkerton disaster, unmeasurable in terms of pain and suffering, already top $60 million. The final tally, most of it being borne by provincial taxpayers, will likely show an amount closer to $150 million – $30,000 for each man, woman, and child in the town. But who's counting?

At Stonegate, Night of the Storm is doing well. The Biesenthals tend their cows and crops and feel like they farm in a fishbowl. They now think less about leaving the land and yellow-brick farmhouse they love. In Hanover, a newborn baby boy gurgles. Peter and Esther Raymond again have a child. The Saugeen River flows ever westward.

Acknowledgements

THIS BOOK would not have been possible had it not been for the solid support of my employer, The Canadian Press. Special thanks to Eric Morrison, Scott White, Paul Woods, Lee-Anne Goodman, and Wendy McCann, to Peter Cameron for his title suggestion, and to Ron Poling for providing the quality CP photographs, taken by some of the best news photographers in North America. Of course, neither their pictures nor my words would have been printed without McClelland & Stewart. Thanks to president Doug Gibson, and to Jonathan Webb, not only for recognizing the value of this undertaking, but for his excellent guidance and exceptional editing. A huge nod, too, to Heather Sangster for an outstanding copy edit.

To my media colleagues for whom Walkerton was not just another story, congratulations on a job well done. It is through the fine reporting of people such as Kate Harries of the *Toronto Star* and Dave Seglins of CBC Radio that Canadians came to understand at least some of what happened. Your work kept me on my toes. A special mention must go to Brent Davis of the *Record*, a young news photographer who discovered he's a darn fine reporter as well. CKNX radio deserves credit for its extensive coverage of the tragedy and aftermath that served its listeners in and around Walkerton so well.

So many people have, in smaller or larger ways, contributed to the creation of this book. To those who indulged my enthusiasm for the undertaking, thank you for listening. Brendan Howley, who did more than listen: your insights and encouragement were invaluable. To freelance reporter Pat Halpin, my favourite Bruce County girl, your help is much appreciated, your friendship special.

In presenting some of the fascinating history of the town and area, I have drawn freely from the work and anecdotes of Lloyd (The Cordwainer) Cartwright, whose wife, Marie, makes the best cream of carrot soup I've ever had, as well as on Norman Robertson's *History of the County of Bruce*. Dale Wilson added some historical perspective and, as importantly, compiled the index. John Finlay helped me with the ground-level view of the town, while Phil Englishman provided a solid overview from his small plane.

To Jeanette, Shary, Kayla, and Danielle, thanks for putting up with my babbling and absences and for being proud of me. I love you.

Many people in Walkerton wanted no part of this. With an ongoing police investigation and judicial inquiry, it's not hard to see why. For some, the pain remains all too fresh even now. But many did share with me their stories, their thoughts, their hopes, fears and tears. It was a privilege and I hope you have not misplaced your trust. It was a treat being invited into your homes and helped make the many months I spent in town that much more pleasant. Your community has a special place in this big-city boy's heart.

Finally, there is little doubt that without the skill, tireless determination, and sensitivity of Dennis O'Connor and his judicial inquiry team, the complete story of the Walkerton tragedy would likely never have emerged (and a snowbound motorist might have spent a whole lot longer in a ditch). They are owed an immense debt of gratitude because it is only through knowing what happened that, as we all so fervently hope, there might never be another Walkerton.

Index